The New Social Control

The Institutional Web, Normativity and the Social Bond

Michalis Lianos
Translated by Richard Nice

RED QUILL BOOKS

I0128240

© Red Quill Books Ltd. 2012
Ottawa

www.redquillbooks.com
ISBN: 978-1-926958-17-0

Printed on acid-free paper. The paper used in this book incor-
porates post-consumer waste and has not been sourced from
endangered old growth forests, forests of exceptional conserva-
tion value or the Amazon Basin. Red Quill Books subscribes to
a one-book-at-a-time manufacturing process that substantially
lessens supply chain waste, reduces greenhouse emissions, and
conserves valuable natural resources.

Library and Archives Canada Cataloguing in Publication

Lianos, Michalis

The new social control : the institutional web, normativity
and the social bond / by Michalis Lianos.
Translation of: Le nouveau contrôle social.

Includes bibliographical references and index.
ISBN 978-1-926958-17-0

1. Social control. I. Title.

HM661.L5313 2012 303.3'3 C2012-901040-5

Originally published as: *Le nouveau contrôle social: toile institutionnelle,
normativité et lien social* by Editions L'Harmattan, Paris, 2001

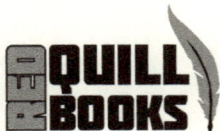

THE QUILL BOOKS

RQB is a radical publishing house.
Part of the proceeds from the sale of this
book will support student scholarships.

Preface to the English edition

This is in many ways an unconventional book. I use micro-sociology and criminology to support sociological theory and I seek to combine unrelated aspects of everyday life into a continuous line of understanding post-industrial society. Although we often tend to focus on the most impressive expressions of technology in order to grasp their impact on society, I have firmly focused on what we still recognize as technological devices but in a banal way: subway tickets, CCTV or burglar alarms. The reason is that there is little in our late modern lives that we do not consider as either innovative or taken for granted; the in-between space can help us understand how institutions weave the web on which our relations increasingly depend.

The overall argument of the book is simple: institutions, that great social invention, are now so developed that they change the sense and form of social relations. Social control used to limit these relations and make them homogeneous, a phenomenon that we used to understand as "conformity". Now, conformity becomes heterogeneous since each institutional environment has its own separate codes of practice and meaning. From a world of communities watching over our entire life trajectory we came to a world of specialised environments that are interested in a particular slice of our existence at a particular moment. These "anthropomoments", as I call them, seem to make our lives unintelligible outside the huge institutional web that capitalist democracy has given rise to. Clustering our individuality around some meaningful, recognizable dimension of ourselves and reassuring each other that we are still decent people that do not mean harm becomes increasingly difficult. We are free and individual enough to be mutually unknown and, inevitably, suspicious of each other.

Fear is at the centre of my approach since I am convinced that all sorts of uncertainty and insecurity come with the experience of the deeply individualised existence of capitalist democracies. But I do not see fear as a consequence of 'new risks'; I see it as a consequence of individual competition in conditions of slow-growth capitalism. Having worked on social fears since my PhD thesis, I think that the "risk society" is essentially the visible consequence of the atrophy of human sociality as we knew it since the Neolithic 'revolution'[1]. This development is closely related to capitalism, which I see as the lowest common denominator of our individual weaknesses. Via capitalism, we continue to flee the constraints of community and seek individual independence even if the price to pay is ubiquitous institutional processes governing every aspect of our lives. And this is the point where control and freedom merge as we choose to adhere to one or another option proposed by the institutional web. We are free to buy this or that good, to use this or that service, to build this or that lifestyle, to adopt this or that identity, but do all this we must. There is no space for mere being, for there

---

1   I have collected much empirical evidence on this via the comparative EC research project "Uncertainty and Insecurity in Europe" and looked at new angles in other international projects.

is no space for inert belonging to a community. There is no irrevocable belonging, no certain position in the post-industrial society. The more the world is controlled and planned, the less each individual can be certain of his or her position.

Eleven years after its publication in French, I hope that this book remains unsettling. In private discussions, some colleagues expressed the view that things cannot be as I describe them because "it would all be too pessimistic". But pessimism, or optimism for that matter, is neither an objective category nor a regulator of knowledge. Moreover, there is nothing pessimistic about leaving "traditional" social control behind us and moving to a new arrangement of social regulation. Communities are ferociously conformist, a fact often brushed aside by today's nostalgia for a return to an imagined idyllic community life. The problem of the institutional web is rather the lack of certainty in social belonging and the lack of stability in one's position and experience, and there is nothing to say that it is impossible to politically impose that stability as part of the "new social control". Politics is in the last analysis the conscious governance of human sociality and I hope that this book helps in asking the appropriate political questions for today's capitalist societies.

Acknowledgements

I would like to thank Nicolas Carrier of Carleton University, Ottawa who was instrumental in making this publication possible. Being very bad at publishing my work, I am sure that without his help this translation would have never seen the light of day. I would also like to thank my editor, George Rigakos, for his patience. Lysette Boucher-Castel, Robert Castel and Jacques Donzelot have encouraged my efforts and my colleagues in Rouen, Catherine Peyrard and Martine Blanc have been very supportive. I deeply thank them all.

Contents

Preface to the French Edition

As I was writing the last part of this essay in December 1999, the media were expressing astonishment at a paradox: the people demonstrating against the World Trade Organization (WTO) meeting in Seattle, Washington were heterogeneous. There were several groups with different aims and priorities, ranging from protection of South American turtles to fair trade; they were protesting against liberal capitalism, while adorned with its most typical products – designer shoes, mobile phones, portable stereos, laptop computers and so on. But, once again, the world's media had missed the real news: the protesters were making a link between every problem on the planet and an organization that was supposed to define and impose rules of interaction among the great institutions of the contemporary world. For them, nothing stood between the individual and the global institution, at least nothing powerful enough to override the close relationship between the two. The Seattle protest should be seen as the official seal of the death for community sociality and the collective forms that underpinned it. It showed that henceforth it would be institutions, both private and public, that hold the keys to postindustrial conditions; institutions would regulate the conditions and distribute their benefits according to their own rules and interests.

The question I raise in this book addresses the mechanisms of this change in practice and consciousness, which has fully immersed social relationships in the mediation of private and public institutions. How did we so readily leave behind the old world of close relationships governed by moral values, governed in their turn by the balance of power between the classes and the political expressions of that balance? How does this new world of indirect sociality build norms, rules of compliance, and thereby deviance? Why, instead of asking everyone to behave legally, do we simply seek to identify and avoid those who might be dangerous? Why do we feel increasingly vulnerable while the institutional web in which we move becomes progressively dense and makes our environment ever more secure and predictable? These questions are quite difficult to tackle separately. However, the great challenge they seem to present is to bring to light their interdependence. This is why I chose to start my exploration of post-industrial sociality and organization from the angle of control. This enabled me to address in what follows a broad spectrum of contemporary questions, from the relationship between social change and technology to traditional social relations, based on the proximity of socialized human beings. The concept of control makes it possible to bring together several problems in a comprehensive approach. This is precisely because at the very centre of late modern societies lies the capacity to control the regulation of relations and the major institutional structures that organize and channel human behaviour. In the future I hope to complete a work on "fluidity" as the primary objective and the ultimate principle of the forms of control that I describe here. That approach will involve the study of new modes of power and stratification brought about by the intense institutionality in which we are starting to immerse ourselves.

I began to develop the arguments presented in this book in Paris, after completing my doctoral thesis, which I was lucky enough to conduct alone, my supervisor being otherwise occupied. I took advantage of this enforced autonomy to theorize post-industrial sociality through its empirical contexts of everyday action and its concrete expressions. In the years following that first work, I found myself in social spaces as different as Greece and Britain, where I often observed that the line of analysis presented here explained and sometimes anticipated the trends of major developments in the relations of post-industrial citizens. My colleagues at the academic conferences where I put forward my vision of the new control gave me some signs of approval. This encouraged me to cease reworking my arguments – by definition an interminable process – and to put them forward here.

I would like to thank Sylvie Perrin for her assistance during the preparation of this work; she has supported me through the long periods of doubt and anxiety that it entailed. I would also like to thank Mary Douglas for her critical encouragement, and my students at Goldsmiths College, University of London, for the interesting exchanges of views we shared.

September 2000

I. Introduction

This book is the first part of an analysis of late modernity as a society of institutions. My intention is to put forward, and not to demonstrate, some fundamental ideas supported by the everyday social experience in which we all participate. I do not attempt either to accumulate the greatest possible evidence to back up these ideas or to develop a critique of the existing analyses. I think it sufficient to articulate the central strand of a theoretical argument that shapes the understanding of late modernity in accordance with categories that seem useful and effective. Readers who are not interested in the theorization of the contemporary condition are advised to go straight to the last part of this introduction, where they will find the traditional preamble to the chapters that follow.

My aim is to explore the production and management of the contexts that integrate human behaviour into organizational objectives, the premises of these objectives and the consequences to which they lead. This set of causes and consequences develops in the institutional web, which grows denser each day. The notion of institution that I apply to the analysis of contemporary capitalist societies is specific to my argument and broader than the meanings of the term that are current in political science, law or sociology. By "institution," I mean any structure that centralizes human behaviour around its own existence and projects and, in this sense, inevitably configures the fragments of action and thought that are devoted to it, with an impact on the inner, personal and social life of the subjects of these fragments. A business, a public service or a shopping mall are institutions, and so are a computer operating system, a phone network or a transportation system[1]. What creates the institution in late modernity is its connecting function, its concentration of actions and thoughts around itself and therefore its inherent capacity to regulate these actions and thoughts, because it generates them. The density and detail of the control of behaviours, achieved by seduction and useful coordination rather than by force, have the effect that the society of institutions[2] is propelling us into a "great regularization" in which the controlled subject is mainly an active and selective user and consumer.

So one of the main suggestions of this book is that the way we understand social control is obsolete and inapplicable to post-industrial reality. We need to revise several ideas that are taken for granted, such as the self-evident association of control with coercion, with the development and prescription of values or with collective social interaction. The highly institutionalized and mediated post-industrial world has its own way of focusing and coordinating the thoughts and actions of its subjects; instead of concentrating on the props of a socially filtered consciousness that supports the action, it is organized

1   Editor's note: These lines were written some years before the advent of "online social networks" so impressively proved them true.

2   I shall use this term to designate societies characterized by great densification of the institutional web. The institutional mediation that emerges in modernity expresses itself more or less intensely depending on the historical stage the society has reached. The societies of high institutionality are obviously "Western'" societies whose "advanced modernity" is only a symptom of this intense institutionality.

around the action itself. The post-industrial citizen is no longer led to fulfil his social contract by the implantation of beliefs or the generation of behavioural rules arising from spontaneous interaction. Rather, he fulfils a performance obligation that is imposed by institutions and by the systems that surround them and to which his life belongs in slices. All that matters is the compatibility of his action with the immense web of interaction mediated by private and public institutions. The interpretation of this compatibility and its relationship with deontological or more generally ethical prescription is only an accessory recourse in grounding the criticism of those who show themselves deviant or ineffective. Culture ceases to emanate from the direct creation of norms and is transformed into a "socio-cognitive"[3] totality, increasingly guided by the parameters of the socio-technical environments carrying social interaction, and made up of individual thoughts embedded in structural constraints. The channelling of post-industrial activity thus raises the problem of a new control, non-intentional and non-coercive, where the norm lies simply in the subject's skill in extracting what she wants at each moment from private and public institutions and the socio-technical systems that serve them. At a highway toll-gate there is only one effective way to act – pay as quickly as possible and drive on. Long before any coercion or value-based prescription, the norm is here identified with the meaning itself. The new control is precisely a control by configuration of the contexts of action, interaction or

---

3   The distinction between "culture" and "cognition", which arose primarily from the functionalist approach to the social world, refers to the need to distinguish between two analytical perspectives, that of the general sociocultural order and that of the individual's capacity to experience understand and situate herself as an actor in relation to that order (Lave 1988: 91-2). The reference to the "sociocognitive" sphere suggests that in post-industrial society these two orders increasingly merge in a common register governed by its own principles.

observation, which sets the terms in which its subject, i.e. its user, perceives and understands these contexts. It is thus based on collaboration obtained by consensus, on the generation of a meaning common to the controllers and the controlled, and not on management of the divergence or resistance that the latter might develop. It exists as a parameter of relationships and is constituted in a neutral way by formalized procedures and protocols of interaction that regularize the similar and parallel behaviours of the participants.

The extraordinary power of this neutral, collaborative control lies in the programmed unfolding of the routines that "process" the individual by embedding her choices in a context of coordination and predetermined options. Acceptance of this context has become a precondition for social participation. The subject plays her various roles by inevitably subscribing to compartmentalized options: the media user chooses at every moment the given content of a TV channel or a Web page; the secretary books a conference room by choosing between empty time-slots; the student selects modules to make up the required number of credits and the user of a washing machine chooses from a set of programs. Control thus becomes one component of post-industrial freedom. It is expressed in the rules for the production and use of the systems, processes and objects that are desirable as means for the autonomous construction of both individual biographies and collective actions. Like the institutional contribution to the relations between individuals and between groups, this control is ubiquitous, deep and growing. The precision with which the regulatory processes insert their rules into the consciousness of their user conveys the prevailing precepts of social life and determines the criteria of acceptable behaviour. That is why we spontaneously tender our ticket to the conductor as he approaches; we recognize our role in a pre-established game. By indicating each time the precise content of "normality," the processes and procedures that make up the new control produce new perceptual, social and legal thresholds that establish the definition of deviance. To refuse the available choices that trigger prefabricated institutional responses is in itself a socially rejected behaviour. Teenagers who run up the down escalator in a shopping mall, pregnant women who fail to take their ultrasound tests at the prescribed dates and young men who ride their scooters in public parks have one thing in common: they are not taking advantage of an environment designed to serve them and established, by virtue of the benefits it brings, as the object of a conformism that is as widespread as it is unconscious. The mere refusal of these freely available offers suffices to identify the refusers as offenders against established sociality. The post-industrial social ethos emanates precisely from the optimal use of rules that are constantly restated by institutional sources, even if each person chooses his own combination of these sources. The large-scale regularization of behaviours thus produces a precise and radical definition of marginality, since it leads to the immediate identification of a 'normative proletariat' made up of all those who cannot or do not know how to extract anything worthy of sustained effort from contact with the institutions. This proletariat obviously includes people whose socialization has not been sufficiently broad and intense to put them in a reasonable position with respect to the competition and their aspirations; those who suffer from an inherited handicap in the development of their skills for interaction with a multitude of social and technical environments and those who try to regain influence using the old method of imposing systems of values instead of adopting non-value-based fluidity, the ultimate credo of a society run by management systems focused on their fields of action. Such groups may include the children of the old "working class," the inheritors of ways of acting and thinking that are too rigid to be modelled according to the constraints of each moment; the children of immigrants, the inheritors of inappropriate aspirations and limited cultural tools; the advocates of a return to an outmoded normativity, derived from the imposition of socio-ethical visions. It is these people, the "hard men", the outsiders, the fundamentalists and the neo-totalitarians that post-industrial normativity exposes as resistant to the modernization of mediated relationships, to indifferent and efficient fluidity.

Each paradigm of normality naturally establishes its deviant opposite, but the particularity of post-industrial control is that it demands autonomy in the form of compliance. Those who cannot constitute themselves as individual and autonomous subjects are the new deviants. They are condemned to invent collective conflicts among themselves – as young people in poor neighbourhoods do – in order to reconstitute a group belonging. The new deviants haunt the daily lives of their neighbours and motivate all those who have the means to do so to flee from them. There is nothing like the televised image of a revolt in the poor suburbs or the rally of a xenophobic political party to convince the post-industrial citizen that her ultimate civic and social duty is now to lead an ever more isolated existence while collaborating perfectly with the institutions that surround her. This ought to sow some doubts in the minds of those who see post-industrial society as a heterogeneous, ungovernable totality. The conflict between diversity and order, which was self-evident in pre-modern societies, has now been overtaken by the fusion of constraint and freedom that the new control constitutes.

Each form of social control is either efficient or on the decline, and the efficiency of post-industrial control lies precisely in updating the immutable goal of all social regulation – to make the existing relationships appear self-evident. The rise of large-scale institutions, operating on the same principles around the globe, would be neither possible nor sustainable without a normativity regulating the nightmares of the participants. The violence in the poor urban areas lifts the corner of the veil on what a society would be like if private and public institutions had little influence. This fear is the foundation of the new consensual control, under which subjects naturally forget that the source of the decline of earlier forms of control lies precisely in the formidable grip of the institutions themselves. In short, like any other control, post-industrial control makes the powerful indispensable.

I.1 The Structuring of the New Control

The regulatory quintessence of post-industrial society lies in the setting-up and orchestration of systems, conditions, and situations that increasingly colonize everyday life and the experiential world. This seems to have an importance that runs through the domain of social control and bears on the rethinking of sociality itself. There exists today a series of systems and structures that, in the organization of social coexistence, seem to have no other role than to perform a managerial and administrative function in a "neutral" way. In doing so, these systems also become

central components of an emergent, underlying, hegemonic socio-cognitive model, imposed without any
critique. The immediate analytical corollary of these
considerations is that one has to rethink social control
based on what appears self-evident and on its reflection
in contemporary forms of power. Implicitly, this constitutes an exploration of the post-industrial paradigm that
directly addresses the distinctive essence of contemporary
conditions, instead of concerning itself with the projections and continuities of modernity.

The work of Michel Foucault thus appears here only
in the background, mainly through the idea that a coordinated set of actions is by definition governed by multiple
powers. In the Foucauldian universe, this idea gives rise
to several deductions that can be summarized in four
propositions: (a) such a coordinated set of actions generally brings with it coercive consequences that are much
more important than those attributed to it; (b) it imposes
prescriptive constraints that go far beyond the aims of its
original *raison d'être*; (c) it contributes in a fundamental
way to the generation of a subject that is specific to it,
since he is compatible with it; and (d) consequently, the
control of human behaviour is more diffuse, extensive
and deeper than has been supposed. These propositions
have not been accepted in full by all historians of social
control. As examples, I would mention the picture of
the development of punishment in Britain presented by
Garland (1985) or Spierenburg (1984) for an alternative
approach to pre-modern control. These critiques in no
way diminish the great influence of Foucault's vision of the
recent past of normalization and punishment. What is less
encouraging, however, is that, after this updating of the
past, we have not advanced in updating the present. From
the domination-focused perspective of Marx and Weber

on the one hand, based more on the coercive dimension of social control than on its symbolic mediation, and the functionalist perspective of Durkheim on the other, the "discipline" that subjugates the "body" remains to a large extent the only renewal of the theoretical tools in the area of normalization. But, the body, and the soul it was thought to contain, are no longer the object of normalization in post-industrial societies, because they no longer occupy a central place in the interactions on which the mode of social organization depends.[4] The body is no longer either the triumphant bearer of power or the field in which, or the tool with which power is applied. The link between physical strength and a certain degree of power is completely broken and lives on only in a clandestine way as a marginalized factor in relations between the sexes and the generations and in a small part of non-organized violent crime. The body has also lost the physical importance that it had in industrial production. Even when machines do not do everything by themselves, what is needed is not strength but the intellectual efficiency to conceive them and use them to their maximum capacity. At the same time, the body is in decline as a bearer of politics. Demonstrations of presence or physical violence conceived as political acts become largely superfluous under the cold precision of opinion polls. Moreover, the role of the body as a bearer of state power in its military dimension is no less marginalized. Automation is reducing ever further the importance of this dimension, which is losing its last bastion with the arrival of war by

---

4   Chris Doran (quoted by Shields 1991: 94) expresses this development in different terms, and goes a long way to retain the body as the site of the exercise of power: "This... is the action of contemporary power. It doesn't work to punish bodies, or even to discipline them, it now works to encode them....The amazing force of this encoding power is that it works by reducing anything outside the code to nonsense".

remote control. In short, in late modernity, the body is an imperfect machine to which the real, competent actor, the intellect, is inextricably attached. Although my objective is to offer a post-Foucauldian model for the understanding of post-industrial control, I also draw on the two gains that *Discipline and Punish* can bring to the study of contemporary normativity and its social function. These are, on the one hand, a perspective that reconstitutes the correctional and disciplinary act as a praxic articulation of power (Garland 1990:47 and 1992) and, on the other, an analysis of the micro-social environment that attributes a *de facto* character to relations of control.

Further, I set the analysis of the new control in the more general and more complex problematic of modes of existence, of which the great master is indisputably Norbert Elias. His *magnum opus* on the "civilizing process" (2000) reveals power in its capacity to create behaviours and sensibilities, beyond how we knew it from analyses of social stratification. He associates domination with the exercise of power through the hegemony of a paradigm around the development of the self. Control and domination are neither identical nor distinct. They merge in the consciousness induced by the new socioeconomic constraints that each era brings. Just as social pacification substituted the courtier for the knight or the table fork for the sword, so globalized managerial fluidity calls for sensibilities that favour the production of subjects who are strategically minded along the whole gamut of their existence, from self-consciousness to the most formal action. Post-industrial sensibilities are focused on the stabilization of a generally predictable but individually unstable world, of which they are products. They are built as responses to institutional guarantees, as expectations of experiences controlled by suppliers external to the person and his immediate circle. They voice the demands of a powerful consumer, immersed in the security and regularity of his preferred services, and for that reason stunned or terrorized by the slightest sign of loss of control. They correspond to a diffuse power, dispersed in things and relationships, which asserts itself by its efficiency and endlessly feeds the expectation of a quick, fluid, orderly unfolding of every kind of development. In the same way that digital bits flow in their billions with infallible precision along fibre-optic cables to their destinations on the other side of the world as quickly and smoothly as to the office next door, so cars are expected to move on highways, trains on their tracks, and people in stores and streets with the same confidence in the configuration of which they are a part. "Incidents," accidents, threats, or assaults are thus transformed: events handled by an emotional or moral normativity, like mourning and blame, have become simply "forbidden" eventualities through the efficient involvement of institutions in all spheres of activity. For the post-industrial being, the victims of a train crash are people who should "normally" be alive; abused children, the homeless, and old people living alone should have been taken care of by the social services; and violent criminals should already have been locked up. The problem of social control no longer presents itself as part of a relationship between human beings, but as a reference to the institutions that govern every aspect of this relationship. Normativity is identified with an extreme sensitivity to disruptions in institutional control and with the strategic preparation that such sensitivity induces. Collaboration in everyday life with the services, schemes and systems that are allied to this demand for security and the greatest possible distance from those who seem different enough to be a threat, are the two main poles of post-industrial normativity.

Just as the prison and the asylum have gone far beyond
the demands that gave birth to them to satisfy the needs
of a new world and to reveal the new tools of power – as
much to the inmates as to outsiders – so self-regularization
and the fear of others lead us into the era of extra-moral,
implicit, non-intentional, and involuntary control. This
control is privatized and fragmented. It marks the transition from a value-based, collective universe, monitored
and strengthened by the state, to the territory managed
and protected by private institutions prioritizing their
own undisrupted functions: the subway, the fast-food
restaurant, the department store, the municipal swim-
ming pool, the office block or even the corner shop
with its CCTV cameras. Outside these territories, there
are only two other poles: vulnerable spaces, nominally
under state control but in reality considered safe only
when relatively frequented; and private spaces of withdrawal into personal and family life, such as the house or
the car. This corresponds to the fact that social control
is now 'delivered' by intermediate systems much more
than it is spontaneously exercised. The normalization of
interaction comes more from preconceived contexts and
widely distributed images than from exchanges between
individuals and groups. We learn to be post-industrial citizens in the theme park and in front of the screen rather
than in the street or the square. We inevitably prefer secu-
ritized contact with others, under the gaze of a guard or
through images, which form the latex glove that protects
us from contamination by the various viruses of social
disintegration. Only in this way can we escape panic in
the face of reputedly ungovernable public housing projects or the constant suspicion that pervades everything
that is not like us. Control and fear become inseparable
in dynamics of mutual reinforcement.

The origins and specific consequences of the new control lie at the heart of socio-technical developments. The high-speed automation of computerized environments makes social negotiation redundant while giving birth to a range of multi-purpose systems that combine functions of management, control, and security. Increasingly established as a ramification of the grip of private institutions on social interaction, the new control is developing along three axes: *privatization, dangerization,* and *periopticity.*

(a) The spaces between the territories managed by private institutions become social vacuums in which individuals accustomed to a guaranteed normativity have no power of control and no wish or capacity to assert rules around themselves. When the guard and the doorkeeper are not present, one must look out for oneself and leave others to their fates. This regression of public normativity reduces the social bond to the level of a mediated relationship and drives the individual to take refuge in the cell of his private life, which thereby constitutes a line of defence. Between the institutional poles of security and the private cell, one has to build bridges – strategic routes between work and home; constant vigilance towards bystanders in the subway; or using the car to deliver the children safely to school. The need to remain constantly in a safe space grows with the fear of exposure to the dangers of public territories, which are increasingly seen as spaces where the law has only a symbolic hold. The conceptual privatization of the illegal act represents primarily the profound erosion of the role played by public institutions in regulating social coexistence. Private institutions thus emerge as the new masters of the world, reforming its norms and shaping relationships in accordance with goals that are alien to social interaction, which has to seek refuge in close, private relationships. The law and the norm are filtered through institutional projects. Those aspects that are useful to these projects will be increasingly applied and reinforced; those that are indifferent or unfavourable will become redundant, because the user is already resigned to the management of normativity by these institutions, and the state has made its choice between the market and dense sociality. This privatization of normativity is not only partial in terms of the identification of undesirable behaviours; it is also selective in its socio-spatial dimension. Poor neighbourhoods can only hope for "regeneration": the opening of shops and supermarkets and the creation of bases for the tracking of norms by private institutions. The existence of the stressed and demoralized local police station simply represents a state that has disengaged from social regulation and from the protection of an explicit model of collective coexistence, even when its intervention is sought. The power behind the control is for the greater part neither sovereign nor administrative, but simply exercised by these poles of convergence, which become by default delegated field agents, ready to impose their own rules of interaction via the detailed configuration of their environments and so to establish their own *pax mercatoria*. These *managed territories* offer the comfort of a controlled sociality and expose the non-managed spaces as effectively unmanageable. The fear aroused by a playground with dilapidated equipment, covered in graffiti and strewn with empty cans, depends largely on the sense of the "clean" and the well ordered that exudes from the nearest fast-food restaurant.

(b) Deprived both of its social support and the sovereign reinforcement of the liberal state, post-industrial control is based less and less on sociocultural systems of values that are becoming ineffective because they presuppose a collectivity on which the post-industrial citizen no longer depends. In the managerial universe that feeds him, his skills in generating values dwindle and are replaced by new useful skills, such as navigating traffic jams, finding a seat in the subway, avoiding dangerous neighbourhoods, and identifying the best offers for cable TV or Internet access. These skills are organized in a "grey efficiency" that does not concern itself with others, except to avoid them. The reproduction of collective values is thus reduced to the rules of politeness that make possible the pursuit of contin-uous and successive relationships with given contexts of action. Practical and isolated coexistence suppresses the margins of diversity that direct social negotiation would have allowed and encourages suspicion and fear. No one negotiates against behaviours that do not fit the principles accepted in pre-regulated environments. Such behaviours characterize people who smoke on the platform and in trains or put their feet on the seat, those who drive cars that throb with the beat of rap music, those who smash up phone booths, those who shove one another or exchange insults, and those who have loud conversations with their friends in the supermarket — in short, those who do not manifest behaviour ostensibly compatible with the norm of the integrated urbanite. These people are neither admon-ished nor punished by others. They are simply avoided, excluded as dangerous and suspect from a game that continues without them. They are represented, analyzed and criticized in the "social" slot of the TV evening news, which deepens their frustration, as much as it sows fear among the rest.

Awareness of the various risks spreads through the tissue of post-industrial society precisely through the vulnerability of individualized experience. In the dread of biographical dangers ranging from unemployment to illness, and of local and global ecological and geopolitical threats, "social risk" takes a central place, based on the fear of others. Here, the danger is constant, real and experienced individually; it can strike in an isolated way and traumatize us in the long term while everything around remains unchanged. The "other" becomes the suspected bearer of a threat that we try to counter by "watching out." Vigilance in everyday movements is incumbent upon all of us and arms us with almost subconscious habits that respond to the dangers of contact. Part of the essential learning of every post-industrial citizen is knowing how to invent and follow in daily life a series of rules that guarantee a viable level of security – knowing which types of individuals are particularly to be avoided, where to sit in the subway, which route to take on foot or by car depending on the time and day of the week, how to avoid being isolated in case of danger, etc. The social world turns, in a banal way, into a terrain of potential threats.

This process of *dangerization* refers to a state of consciousness detached from experience and raised to the order of a given social condition. Paradoxically, it is the high level of security of the post-industrial subject that encourages him to dangerize his world. While the actual dangers may be reduced, the tolerance for dangers is also diminished. Thus, the management of every natural, technical, and social aspect of the environment exemplifies and confirms an ever more advanced, more innovative and more modern society. There are no longer any truly "natural" disasters after the development of the ecological consciousness and no more unaccountable hazards now that the railroad companies offer compensation for delays. Undesirable changes are breaches in institutional obligations, errors in analysis, standardization, strategy, or implementation. It is impossible to resist the world of institutional activity, not to project its securitization onto individual or family existence. However, at this level, institutional constraints are no longer valid and the "other" ceases to be a salesperson, civil servant, shopkeeper, janitor, or artist. He becomes unknown and obscure by being able to act without the institutional weight on his shoulders, and so breaks the promise of a contact guaranteed by systems that go beyond him. His dangerization thus relates to the reading of the signs that might link him to such a system, and, which would therefore limit the potential threat. It is the sign of a weak or non-existent link with an institutionalized context that initially arouses the fear of victimization and becomes the centre of social dangerization. A person who flaunts his non-membership of institutional securitization becomes the model of social dangerousness, a likely perpetrator of phobogenic crimes, a refractory and thereby threatening subject of post-industrial control. From this point of view, fear of victimization is the peak of post-industrial dangerization, and security devices are its most prolific generators.

(c) Post-industrial control consists of new ways of developing and imposing prescriptions for behaviour. The privatized and dangerized management of social relations no longer obeys the principles introduced by modernity. This is as valid for the prison and the army as for public spaces. The panoptic prototype of a single, centralized mode of surveillance is now obsolete and ineffective. The post-industrial world bases its control, as much as the management of the worlds it colonizes, on autonomous action. This is not a contradiction, but a necessity in an environment of social interaction served by socio-technical systems and by large-scale private and public institutions. Human action, in work, consumption, transportation, or entertainment is managed and tracked by a web of structures sufficiently dense and regularized to be able to determine the content of social existence. Control is here a *de facto* element, since subjects are normalized by the growing refinement of the skills that seem useful to them. In other words, the large scale of institutional management imposes its rules so far upstream that daily action contrary to them becomes an absurdity more than a challenge; in a highly regularized world, driving the wrong way on a one-way street or trying to enter a building through the automatic exit door is simply a waste of time. Because routine tasks are computerized and run by action protocols, the demands on the subject relate not to blind compliance, which is of little use in the circumstances, but to displaying initiative, which demonstrates social aptitude. Teachers, employers, prison governors and social workers are all interested in the autonomous performance of the subjects over whom they exercise power – the independence of thought and action these subjects show in their relationships with institutions. Post-industrial control is not oriented toward mere surveillance but towards autonomous, differential, and therefore, individualizing motivation.

The institutional structures surrounding the post-industrial citizen often compete for her attention and her involvement in their projects. This competition, very obvious in the consumption and entertainment sectors, is no less intense elsewhere. Interpellation by advertising is only one example of the battle of private and public institutions to occupy the thematic compartments of individual life, which they target in their activities. The difference between the daily efforts of the media to catch the attention of viewers and the leaflet from the town hall that explains how to dispose of bulky refuse is quantitative. The post-industrial subject is deluged with institutional messages that constantly point out ways of thinking and acting that give priority to prefabricated action projects. The dizzying proliferation of choices, but always choices of joining in or signing up, represents the currently established science of freedom. Far from being a centralized surveillance, social control emerges in these circumstances as an apprenticeship in compliance around several competing poles. The subject is obliged to choose his own range of involvement but must exist and act by conforming independently and intelligently to the multitude of institutional poles. He is propelled into a perioptic environment where the strength of the norm depends on the adherence it can arouse, which itself depends on the attraction that the institutional messages and practices can exert. It is no longer the brute strength of a centre inculcating compliance that controls contemporary subjects, but the capacity to attract their gaze, which, by this common but atom-ized focusing, establishes and legitimizes their point of convergence as a *de facto* centre of normativity. Perioptic control is rooted in the parallel individuality of subjects that no longer need to be artificially isolated. Cellular-ized by their own experience, they comply with what their convergence establishes as accepted and therefore, prescribed. The institution becomes a *periopticon*, i.e. a point of multiple foci, and so a place of socialization, without having wished it and without being interested in this function. Whether it be a Hollywood star, an industrial conglomerate, an Internet search engine or a department store chain, the convergent individual gazes and practices are neither offered nor received on a moral or even value-based foundation; they simply represent a massive utility in liberal capitalism. From this point of view, perioptic control deepens the desocialization of the norm by propagating itself in ever wider circles and very clearly breaks with any coercion.

I.2   The Socio-cognitive: Legitimacy, Inspection, Technology

The new control introduces rules, the rationale and content of which do not derive from some social deontology. The long line inaugurated by Plato's *Laws*, making individual action a source of community utility, has come to an end. If Socrates drinking the hemlock exemplifies the sociogenesis of the rule, the post-industrial actor draws the legitimacy of his action from the configuration of the socio-technical environments that surround him: everything that is possible is allowed; everything that is allowed is legitimate. Both the normal and the deviant are determined by references to a social ethos representing more the approval of the institutions than the relations between actors. The legitimation of action is not in the hands of its author, who, although not directly controlled, is constantly required to make his acts compliant with the demands of the institutional web in which his life unfolds. Often, he must offer in advance access codes that guarantee this compatibility, such as the passwords and digits needed to enter his building, use his bank card or watch a film on cable TV. The knowledge legitimating this access is not subject to cultural constraint. Independent of interaction, it introduces secrecy as the key element of the action. What is important is by definition something to be protected from others rather than to be accepted by them. Suddenly, social regulation is built more on atomization than on collectivity. The legitimate used to be conceived as

a sphere that was often produced by, and necessarily mani-
fested in, the cultural order; it crystallized as a formal rule,
a norm, a belief, an opinion, a habit, a mentality or more
generally as social know-how. From the primary, monolithic imposition by violence to the multitude of voluntary
positionings, legitimacy was constructed precisely through
concrete situations that carried the cultural within them,
or around which one hoped to organize the cultural in a
way that made these situations acceptable to the societies
in question. This cultural appeal to social interaction is
now unnecessary.

Access to institutional spaces, services, and guarantees
is the basis of a new mode of socio-cognition that one would
hesitate to call a culture. This mode replaces negotiation
with adherence, beliefs with parameters, and hierar-
chies with levels of access. It establishes the legitimacy of
behaviour as a skilled compliance that now reproduces
itself individually in its isolated relationships with institutions and which takes on a specifically social meaning
only through its homogenizing dissemination. Perioptic
convergence breaks the old premises of social regulation,
based on the unavoidable mediation of consciousness, and
introduces the new rules of socio-cognitive reproduction
based purely on compliant action. Thus, the social bond is
reduced to the status of a common learning of experiences
organized and managed by institutions. The demand for
intellectually active participation to establish and maintain the hegemonic paradigms of social life has negligible
impact if it does not correspond to the map of institutional options. Opinions are uttered one-directionally in
opinion polls, market research surveys and the media,
i.e. only where they have a chance of influencing this
map. There is nowadays little meaning to the prescriptive
acceptance or rejection of behaviours and lifestyles: when

a media empire decides that a program for devotees of "gangsta rap", piercing, or partner swapping is a profitable market niche, when a fast-food chain associates itself with violent films and video games, it is perfectly impossible to contain this development, since the calculation of public opposition has already been made, and very often quite accurately. So, one coexists with those who are different, on parallel tracks of experience, as consumers of other options that suit us better but which are not more legitimate; and one seeks to widen the range of those options that legitimate one's own niche of existence. When your favourite café allows you to live out your homosexuality in public, when your bakery offers a low-calorie sandwich to suit your chosen diet, and your employer prevents smokers from damaging your health, what is the meaning of a specifically social negotiation about sexual preference, the aesthetics of the body or passive smoking? It is much more practical to set up a direct dialogue between self-identity and its institutional suppliers. The post-industrial citizen addresses himself to and complies with those who speedily fulfil his needs, rather than taking the uncertain route of social influence. It is as inevitable a choice as its everyday expressions; you don't borrow from a friend, because the ATM is faster, more discreet and always available. As a result, the loop of institutional configuration of the social universe is closed with the recognition that what works is by definition legitimate.

This circle of legitimacy objectivized by action suits all its participants but provides no place for those who cannot constitute themselves as participants. One could define contemporary social exclusion as a state of non-integration into the institutional environment and deviance as non-compliance with this environment. Those who cannot become efficient and docile users of the institutional web suffer an automatic and radical segregation simply because they do not present sufficient signs of attachment to this network, and, therefore, of dependence, guaranteeing their regulated participation in the atomized game that surrounds them. Likewise, the success of this game depends on the inability of the excluded to set up another one. Those who transform this incapacity into a condition of voluntary opposition are the only ones who visibly threaten the direct dialogue between the individual and institutions. Therefore, they find themselves confined in the midst of a world of frenetic exchange. That is why post-industrial control has real meaning only as a preventive and integrating treatment. Punishment, especially imprisonment, can be seen as failure in a world that exerts its control through the proliferation of choices rather than by disciplinary subjection. The regularization of contacts and processes carries a constant preventive inspection. Little importance is attached to this development because it is regarded as self-evident; this is why we have no conceptual framework addressing changes in the channelling and control of behaviour at the end rather than the beginning of the 20th century. It also explains why all attempts to adapt the existing concepts, such as the "dispersal of discipline" thesis (see the essays by Bottoms, Cohen, Mathiesen and Scull in Garland and Young 1983; also, Shearing and Stenning 1985) come up against the fact that the new forms of social control are not there to control but to configure an environment of voluntary interaction, and the fact that they do not form part of a truly "social" control.

To respond to these two paradoxes, the general concept of "social control" has to be replaced by a *control in advance, conducted on predetermined criteria and in relation to acts taking place in a context of institutions.* These controlling activities cluster around their inspecting character, i.e. a querying of the act that bears on the actor and her compliance or non-compliance with the rules. Clearly, inspection is a divisible category. The range of acts of inspection is truly immense – from the doorkeeper's gaze to the CCTV camera in a store, from the parking attendant's scrutiny of permits to the receptionist's polite question, from a line manager's call for a report to the credit company's request for bank statements, from the call on an entry phone to the request for ID. What all these acts have in common is that, in one way or another, they *question* the subject, i.e. they require a behaviour. And, in so doing, they *recommend* to the subject of this behaviour a course of action that takes place within well-defined limits. It must be stressed that these limits have an institutional origin: the doorman and not the neighbour, the bank clerk and not the friend, the line manager and not the colleague. From this standpoint, inspection can be seen not as a distinct form of social control, but as its development in the conditions of late modernity.

Atomized autonomy, the symptom and cause of the embedding of the social in formalized relationships,[5] makes an act of inspection a hybrid act that also refers to social values and the social ethos, but which mainly operates by reinforcing these values only insofar as they serve precise institutional interests.[6] In this sense, the universe of inspection is made up of acts and processes that not only carry a socially grounded authority, but also shape

---

5   Giddens (1990:59) sees this institutionalization as the quintessence of developments in the evolution of modernity.
6   The typical opening question of a receptionist, "How can I help you?" is a good example of the multiple ends achieved through the act of inspection. The question contains at once the assertion of the importance of the institution, it places the burden of legitimation on the side of the addressee, it meets the obligation to serve a client, and provides the speech act to initiate communication.

their social context into precise forms and establish conditions that facilitate and deepen the inspecting function.

These tendencies are better understood when it is borne in mind that the actor has no option regarding the inspection. He is subjected to it by virtue of asking for something that imposes inspection as a qualifying stage that is either formally required or triggered by his individual situation. It may be a contractual requirement (such as an obligatory medical examination for an insurance contract); more often, the inspection is inextricably embedded in what is requested (using a ticket for public transportation, providing personal data to subscribe to a service, etc.). The great majority of the acts and processes of inspection are not imposed by law but are legally optional; they are part of "everyday life," the field of action that the law leaves to the discretion of society. From this point of view, an act of inspection is an underlying act of domination, an invisible and thereby efficient application of a social logic of preventive control. In the chapters that follow, I try to show how such a logic is diversified to reach the different levels of social experience, but it is also important to know that these diversifications are only the differentiated expressions of a single original fear – loss of control over a field of action or a territory managed by the institution concerned in each case. That is why the inspecting approach to contact with the user begins at the moment of first encounter and is thereafter constantly reapplied in small doses. This continuously underlines who is required to prove the legitimacy of his presence or request, who is the visitor and who is the host. The user's behaviour thus ends up integrating itself into the model imposed by the process or space that it enters, which results in the immediate identification of those who threaten these processes and spaces. One of the major uses of inspecting control is to identify the defiant with the deviant and so eliminate any possible route for legitimate but non-compliant behaviours. The inspecting control establishes a binary and monosemic world, made up of friends or foes and having meaning only in relation to the unfolding of the activity concerned in each case. Unlike the correcting control of our properly social environment, inspecting control is barely interested in the whole, long-term behaviour of each individual. The individual exists only insofar as he is present, and he is controlled on each new occasion in the same way, with the same intensity; there is no leniency for previous good conduct. One is no less checked at the airport security gate the nth time one goes through it than the first; and there is no point in claiming that one has many times come to an office building for a meeting with someone who works there. Inspecting control thus prevents the actor from accumulating a durable legitimacy for his actions or assimilation into his environment. Unlike the corrective control generated by social proximity that intervenes to re-establish a broken compliance, the new control addresses behaviour in a formative way. Its precise repetitions, which each time reset the social counter to zero, imply no relationships; they set up functional collaborations that are always temporary and immediately retractable, even when they are renewed over a long period and create the illusion of continuity. This can only lead to a fragile, volatile universe, in which reserves of certainty are rapidly exhausted in the quest for constant renewal of links and statuses that already constitute the greater part of the socialized self.

The new control still fulfils the historical functions of all forms of social control: it imposes and reinforces a social ethos, favouring the established distribution of power; but this does not suffice to explain its binary preventive nature, which depends mainly on the forms of interaction and the means used to make that distribution of power materialize. This is where technology makes a crucial contribution. It offers the planning prototype on which the new control deploys its own canvas. There are some fairly spectacular novelties one might single out to support the thesis of a radical break between a pre-informatic and a post-informatic control. For example, what equivalent can one find in the past to the electronic tag that guarantees its wearer's presence within a certain radius (Mair and Nee 1990), or a system that records a reader's entries to and exits from a library?[7] While the importance of such direct applications is not to be denied, they must be seen in a larger context that views technology as a social function directly impacting post-industrial socio-cognition. The important change is not the application of new technologies to security purposes, but the immersion of contemporary experience in an archipelago of socio-technical environments and systems, giving rise to a new sociality that blurs – and often wipes out – the boundaries between control and freedom, action and passivity, participation and isolation, and a whole series of categories that seemed self-evidently distinct until the second half of the twentieth century. This new socio-cognition follows the operating principles of the great socio-technical ensembles that are reorganizing the socioeconomic universe by controlling its development as much as they generate it. Therefore, control is no longer made up of the constraints imposed on an activity external to it, but rather of the parameters and safety valves that, essentially with the aid of information technologies, become pre-conditions for that activity. The constant monitoring for risk reduction is a perma-

---

7   Most public and university libraries are now equipped with such a system.

nent parameter incorporated in all areas of concentrated activity – stock exchange, nuclear power station, highway, stadium, airport, or city centre. Control is applied on the same precautionary and predictive principle through the spectrum of activities concerned and disseminates the logic of early isolation of elements associated with danger. The use of automated technical means thus homogenizes the contribution of control, and technology becomes the institutional spearhead in the battle against the diversity of behaviours that, by its nature, complicates and slows the game. Socio-technical environments that substitute the configuring of action and interaction for direct sociality[8] would never have been possible without an information technology that can individually monitor the growing number of users. The more this technology evolves, the more control will take on its forms and use its principles. More than any other factor, it is the routine incorporation of technology in everyday life that will influence the definition and treatment of danger and deviance in the decades to come. It is not a question of a technological revolution in the area of control, for, as Larochelle (1991: 328) observes, "the notion of technological revolution does not exist in reality, except as a reifying designation of absolute objects; it is therefore not a heuristic but an ideological category." Rather, it is an adaptation to technical means that are advantageous in terms of time and cost, projecting new models of compliance that are more distant and compartmentalized but also more rigid. The transition from a culture based on beliefs and values to a socio-cognition fed by the institutional and technical configuration of the social world cannot exclude norma-

---

8   This term is used here to cover the great historical range of 'traditional' social relationships not configured by impersonal institutionalized environments; I oppose direct sociality to an increasingly mediated "institutional sociality."

tivity as it progresses. Inspection replaces law, prevention replaces accusation, danger replaces the offence, and predetermined options replace diversity, as much in normality as in deviance.

I.3 Summary of the Arguments

In the *second chapter*, I examine the social dynamics of a subway ticket. As Norbert Elias (2000: 411) puts it, "to investigate the totality of a social field does not mean to study each individual process within it. It means first of all to discover the basic structures that give all the individual processes within this field their direction and their specific stamp." The reader is therefore invited to extend and adapt my observations to the growing number of devices and structures involving the inspection and regularization of their users' behaviour, such as computer programs and networks, sites of mass consumption, or the systems regulating urban traffic.[9] My observations on the subway system aim to reveal some immense transitions in both praxic and cultural structures that are often too close to be noticed. I use the subway as the typical example[10] of the convergence of banal everyday experience in post-industrial cities, but I shall not consider here the meaning of an underground transport network in the context of the debate on late

---

9   There is a need to counterbalance in some way the reluctance of the "human" sciences to recognize the machine (or at least the intelligent machine) concretely as a technogenous social actor. This reluctance is no doubt part of the long anthropocentric obsession that still pervades the study of society and sometimes reduces it to an analysis of individual choices. In this sense, it is worth noting that the world of objects remains excluded even in the context of disciplines closer to psychology (Leeds-Hurwitz 1989: 105).

10   In a spirited description, Marc Augé (1995) uses the term "non-places" to designate the areas of "accelerated circulation of persons and goods" that are increasingly frequent in post-industrial societies. These non-places precisely exemplify the deep changes in contemporary experiences.

modernity.[11] Instead, I concentrate on the meaning of small actions; repetitive, automated learning; and the self-evident reflexes of the users. These reflexes define a large part of the public existence of post-industrial citizens and include a dynamics of action and comprehension that runs through their conception of the social bond. The grip of a great socio-technical structure on the human flows that it governs introduces new parameters of legitimation and creates thresholds between the world of the device and the external world. All negotiation becomes impossible, because the system imposes on the user its binary logic, identifying the perfectly acceptable and the perfectly unacceptable. This new legitimacy is distributed by the device according to its own criteria, which proportionally weakens the scope of the social criteria used in a context of non-mediated human interaction. Developments of this order corrode the sociality of direct contact with an important repercussion on its normative and value-based content. Socio-technical and institutional mediation thus reveals itself as the root of the decline of hegemonic values and identities.

The demise of "decent people" and their replacement by actors identical in their action and diversified in their consciousness also raises new problems for the study of control. It is a simple common sense observation: the

---

11 The scale and complexity of the technical systems introduced by modernity have several times been identified as sources of transformation of the consciousness of space-time and social relations. To isolate this type of structure, which lies beyond the user's knowledge and control over the functioning of the system, several terms have been used, emphasizing particular consequences in each area. Whereas Giddens (1991) speaks of "expert systems," stressing the user's confidence, Alain Gras (1993) refers to "technical macrosystems" to emphasize the autonomy of their rationality and the novelty of the lived experience associated with them. See also the thesis of Habermas (1970) on the connection between the development of "goal-oriented" (*zweckrational*) systems and modernization.

subway turnstiles are not responsive to the good manners, prestige or radiant beauty of the possible user. In a social universe where all the material and behavioural parameters associated with the individual have become the objects of minute and extreme class evaluations, one discovers some very influential mechanisms that initially seem to oppose this dominant equilibrium. Two apparent paradoxes are involved: first, access control devices are at the same time temples of a "pure" equality, devoid of social bias and prejudice; second, this development is a historical novelty, constantly pursued for at least twenty five centuries, but now dismissed with indifference. We certainly need a new debate on the nature and consequences of transitions that are centered on the performance of institutions and the technical devices that serve them. If technocentric equality is a reality, it is also true that selective detection focuses on rejection; it transmits an inverted logic in which the granting of a positive status is only the negation of a negative status. Before moving to the level of the distribution of power and social stratification, this new debate must therefore take account of regularization as a life principle of post-industrial society. It must also take account of the new factors of social differentiation created by the proliferation of structures that regularize contemporary activity by excluding in advance all those who are not able or willing to follow.

In the *third chapter*, the question of regularity is explored entirely through the examination of systems that track and memorize signs of behaviour. The message of a regularizing device to its targeted population lacks variance. Behaviours are channelled into preconceived, rigid pathways and the internalization of this channelling is performed through "learning by doing." However, there exist some less rigid interactive contexts that are, nonetheless, monitored and regulated by the institution that reigns there, such as the department store, the theme park, the supermarket, or the office block. The subtlety of the control of these spaces comes through the involvement of the participant in the regularizing processes. Among several other – ever more numerous and complex – devices, the CCTV camera now exemplifies the establishment of a control of the participant by himself, due to his awareness of an external gaze.

The camera does not prevent acts; it prevents decisions. As a purely deterrent instrument, it relies on its target to realize the specific meaning of the gaze applied at each moment. It sets up a game in which appearing normal consists in aligning oneself with other users and seeking not to stand out and so attract the presumed gaze of the camera. The regularization is here comparative, growing, and self-imposed and enlists its target as an actor in his own surveillance. I use the term "hyper-regularity" to emphasize that this process can only generate centripetal tendencies resulting in a growing homogeneity of behaviours. This tightening of the limits of the normal arises from the simple fact that the participants avoid adopting behaviours on the periphery of the conformist majority, because, albeit permitted, these behaviours are more likely than others to arouse the suspicion of the device. The peripheries are thus deserted and progressively delegitimized. Other differentiations will be revealed as a consequence, leading in their turn to a new reinforcement of the centre.

Hyper-regularity is founded secondarily on two other aspects of the device. First, the participant becomes an actor on the security stage, because surveillance renders him both suspect and protected. The device dangerizes its field and diffuses the awareness of a threatened environment. It points to the other users, since those who represent the real danger must by definition be among them. Second, the recorded image strips the act of its unique time of performance and makes it reproducible. The remoulding of the past, that ultimate tool of social integration, thus gives way to the certainty of a constant and indisputable present that is sure to persuade any jury more than skilful arguments that might otherwise have sown doubts. The whole set of these developments completes the transition to an intense regularization of the forms of public sociality. The inevitable result is a very broad definition and an increased fear of anything that does not fit into this well-managed homogeneity.

In the *fourth chapter*, I examine the binary polarization between the normal and the abnormal, and the fear of others that this polarization invariably generates through different social environments. How is a situation constructed in which violent crime becomes the factor of a major and multiple social dichotomy: between men and women, young and old, rich and poor, light and dark skinned, city-dwellers and suburbanites, or conservatives and socialists? The management of perceptions through the media is of course subject to its own dynamics of exaggeration of all dangers. However, the anxiety around "crime" goes far beyond other fears. In contrast to collective industrial and environmental threats, the fear of victimization is constantly experienced in a private and isolated way. Yet, its greatest particularity is that it is the only one that refers directly to the intentions of others. The separation between those who do not have the same income, lifestyle, and culture is deepened by the proliferation of atomized public activities and socially homogeneous private activities. How can one construct this "other" who is not like us, if not through contact with his differences? If we do not meet him at work, in the shopping mall or at the school parents' meeting, he has nothing to offer us; we do not want to know him. One can thus easily represent him massively through his most flagrant and, therefore, most extreme difference. This dangerized "other" exists in our avoidance strategies, not our action strategies, in the fear of being attacked, threatened, or raped.

My aim is not to provide a synthesis of the biases and distortions that lead to this dangerization, but to show how its origins and its consequences, amplified and filtered by the institutional web, lead to new perceptions of crime and control. In line with the increased institutional mediation of social contacts, crime as a legal and public category is disappearing. It is being replaced by a problem of private fear that has to be confronted by the use of protection or avoidance strategies. The logic of regularization is replicated in consciousness and in behaviours, with quick, suspicious glances at others. The prescriptions of compliance no longer bear on a difference, so long as the difference only produces consequences for its own subject. Criminal law has never succeeded in imposing on modernity the principle that "deviant" behaviours causing no concrete harm should be exempted from punishment. For modern societies, always governed through a hegemony of values, this was part of the social bond implying that the "other" should comply with a prescribed normality, extending to the most private matters, such as sexual practices or belief in God. However, what the legal doctrine tried unsuccessfully to introduce has been set up in the space of just a few years as a taken-for-granted condition: private life is opened up to an extreme diversity that interests only its subject. By contrast, the social scope of the individual is constantly evaluated and arouses suspicion at the slightest sign of "external deviance." Contemporary concerns are constructed around protection while abandoning judgement; people are no longer interested in rejecting atheists and homosexuals but in the "fight" against paedophiles and fundamentalists. Deviance is socially defined purely on the criterion of fear. Legality withdraws into the televised world of institutions as one useful category among others, to decide political, economic, or administrative "affairs" and scandals. In the specifically social world, or its contemporary vestiges, all that counts is phobogenic deviance and the strategies for avoiding it. This explains the intense fortification of the private sphere, using both cultural and praxic means to barricade the experience of each individual and each family in a tunnel where one interacts only with those who fear the same dangers. This homogenization based on a hierarchy of fears stratifies the subjects of late modernity according to their efficacy in inoculating their lives against the social pollution of insecurity. Initiatives to make spaces "safe" and "agreeable," schools well-performing and free of violence, and neighbourhoods "attractive" combine in the trademark of the new urban bourgeoisie. The latter is today not so much urban as characterized by its distance from social pollution, by its capacity to use only the spaces and services that it does not want to avoid. I shall try to give indices of this inverted stratification, showing that it is structured differently depending on its cultural foundations, but in order to arrive at the same ends. Whether it is the proliferation of neighbourhood watch schemes, as in the United States; tools for declaring membership of the middle class, as in Britain; or a Republican police securitization, stubbornly blind to the self-evidence of a multicultural society, as in France, the result remains a class symbolism, based on exposure to these dangerous "others." The essential vehicles of social division, such as income, today perform a stratifying function that has more to do with

the fear of victimization than with consumption. This is
not an expression of new needs for social differentiation, a
tendency linked to the multiple lifestyles and identities that
arise from wide access to consumption. On the contrary, it
is a transition that counteracts this tendency by encircling it
with dark, imaginary, primary fears. The creation of whole
neighbourhoods protected by private police forces in the
United States inaugurates a new era in the development
of the social bond and exemplifies the division by fear that
takes its place alongside the division by power. The dangerization of an "other," from whom far fewer things ultimately
separate us than those that separated two successive social
classes at the start of the twentieth century, perfectly exemplifies the new socio-cognitive mode generated by the
institutional management of atomized subjects.

Should it then be concluded that the new control
revives archaic fears using elaborate technical and managerial structures that dominate the societies of advanced
modernity? In reality, the development is much more
important, since it bears on a new mode of coexistence –
distant, parallel and prophylactic. Some old forms of local
control live on in the societies of late modernity; but they
are rapidly being replaced by institutional processes that
motivate, channel, and confine their subject in entirely new
ways. We need to reflect on the foundations of this transition: is the new control a "social" control? The replacement
of collective approval by access to institutions and of nego-
tiated culture by preformatted socio-cognition seems to
suggest that the era of "involuntary" social regulation is
now beginning. The absence of the intention to control
reigns at the same time as the minute detail of the rules.
The aims of the devices are different each time, but they are
achieved by similar principles. Constituted as a membrane
on the institutional web, the new control filters action and

so brings about a new coherence in the consciousness of its subject, which directly affects the structuring of the powers that surround it. Describing and determining the modes of power brought in by the intense institutionalization of the social would require a separate analysis. Inasmuch as control is concerned, I give here in my conclusions some indices of the hyper-regular bio-power of late modernity and its capacity to make what is value-neutral socially productive. This capacity is based on the possibility of a world without values but filled with conventions, standards, and parameters. It is a fascinating perspective, especially in its egalitarian dimension, freed from hegemonic belief systems. But, will the involuntary hegemony that emerges create its own dominated class, segregated from the other classes without being considered at fault or inferior, simply because it will be unable to situate itself where the game is being played? Will the new control lead to the creation of a permanent proletariat without a distinct culture and without an adequate social excuse for their situation, made up precisely of those that no institution seeks to attract and, therefore, to control? In a subversive inversion, the controlled will henceforward be the dominant, those who, labelled by the institutions, possess the proof of good social quality, as an object or service bears the stamp of a standard of production. The uncontrolled will be of unknown quality, hence potentially uncontrollable and, therefore, dangerous and excluded. The new control is thus very likely to propel the class struggle into purely symbolic areas and sharply expose the question that any objective structure of stratification conceals: in what way does the "other" deserve his or her place more (or less) than we do? If regulating mediation attenuates the social bond, it brings with it an immense potential for a more sophisticated and also more honest social dialogue.

II. REGULARITY: THE SUBWAY

Forty years have passed since Robert Nisbet (1971: 47) declared that "technology will significantly affect human behaviour only as it ceases to be something external and becomes internalized in a culture, a recognized part of norms and institutions." For post-industrial societies that time has come. Everyday life mainly consists of acts that have meaning only as elements of systems made possible by technology. The observations that follow focus on the social transmutation that this new stage has induced, and they can probably be seen as an attempt to bear witness to the dawn of the socio-technical era.

Social control in advanced modernity is mainly conceived and concretely exercised by institutions. The voluntary constitution of life trajectories freed from collective constraints is the major social conquest of the post-industrial subject. The "other" has become an autonomous actor to be respected and is less and less a guide or judge of our own actions. The cause and symptom of this tendency, the fact that the social universe relies on private and public organizations for the maintenance of the normative sphere, represents the completion of the decline of direct social relations and the significant deficit of the rules that underlay them. The organizational mode of control is grounded in the structures that configure action toward ends defined and pursued by institutions. The actor integrates herself into the pre-constructed context that is offered each time: the lanes of a highway, the entrances and exits of supermarkets, traffic lights and pedestrian paths, the commands allowed by her software, or the passwords given by her Internet service provider. The world we experience and the world we think about become more like a series of themed environments; one can adopt one or another of them but never change their rules. Less than a century separates the barcodes guaranteeing the weight and price of our favourite preserve from the haggling over quantity and price with the grocer. This new world that reveals itself exclusively by a myriad of "take it or leave it" options, lies beyond us in its efficacy precisely to the extent that it manages us according to a plan that lies beyond our ken. Among these systems managing our day-to-day lives, I have chosen to concentrate here on the Paris subway network. My aim is to avoid the assumption that I am seeking to base the understanding of contemporary forms of control on recent technological innovations, the social implications of which are still uncertain. The experience of the subway – banal, everyday, and undergone *en masse* without being collective – has reigned over the tedium of millions of city dwellers for more than a century. Neither innovative nor particularly backward, it symbolizes "typical" urban life and represents the socially absorbed and taken-for-granted stratum of modernity.

II.1 Legitimation and Negotiability

Things seem simple. Almost mechanically, we walk into a subway station, put our ticket into the machine and go down to the platform; we take the first train, journey to our destination, and take the exit that suits us. We do it "like everyone else does." Is there any reason to think further about it? First point: not everyone gets into the subway. The only people who can enter are those who have a ticket or a pass, i.e. a magnetic strip that fulfils the requirements of a control network.

The turnstiles at the entrance to each station form a legitimation device. Both legally and sociologically, their existence automatically creates a set of natural persons – "actors" for the sociologist – who have the right to be in the protected space. Mere presence beyond the limit set by the machine constitutes the legitimation of the user, because it presupposes it. We thus arrive at a first equation: *physical presence (or simply presence) = legitimated presence.*

What are the unknown quantities in this equation? In other words, how does one attain this automatic dimension of legitimation? A space that everyone can potentially use ("practice," in Michel de Certeau's sense (1984)) is *de facto* a public space. Yet, in spite of its vast extent and its millions of daily passengers, we have here a space of exclusion. The turnstiles, increasingly reinforced with tall doors physically preventing entry without the consent of the machine[12] – are there simply to exclude those who have not paid to use the network. The machine divides the world in two: the accepted, legitimate users, and the external world, excluded from the network. Hence, a second equation: *legitimation = threshold.*

The only element on which the process interrogates the external world is a set of data imprinted in a magnetic language translated by a computer system; in a word, digits. The procedure is based on the control of a message

---

12   The description here is based on the Paris Métro, which assigns employees only to punitive inspections, in contrast to the London Tube, where staff are given the preventive role of watching over the inward and outward flows to "confirm" the operation of the turnstiles, which are less aggressive than those of the Paris network. In either case, it is always the electronics that attributes the legitimate status.

that remains inaccessible to the world outside the network. This leads us to the third and final equation: *selection = encrypted compatibility*.

From the point of view of legitimacy, the first presup-position of the operation of the access control process is the absolute division between persons, the formation of an environment that legitimates user A and not would-be user B, or rather, that separates the population into users and non-users. As regards the social barrier, i.e. the possi-bility of taking part in an activity – in this case, belonging among those who can use a transportation service – we see here the emergence of a new means of legitimizing and delegitimizing an action.

In the first place, the pragmatic reference is a spatial limit that becomes a symbolic limit. There is an extreme clarification of the object of permission, and this is neces-sarily reflected in the structuring of the legitimate, which cannot remain a continuum with several forms and quantitative or qualitative variations, but divides into two equally inflexible parts: legitimate or illegitimate, rather than more or less legitimate. The multiplicity of a scale is transformed into an exclusive duality. This development, arising from technical feasibility, leads to a profound restructuring of the experiential space and its percep-tion, closing the socio-cognitive terrain to practices of negotiation. Nevertheless, a first level of analysis, that of legitimation, is indispensable in order to reach more general conclusions.

To clarify what I mean by the difference between graduated legitimation on the one hand and binary legitimation on the other, I shall use three models of interaction that are at once plausible, hypothetical and habitual in the everyday manifestations of the experi-ential world. These stereotypes are used with the aim of ordering the distinction in question through empirical simulations[13] and not in an explanatory or corroborative sense.

1) Let's begin with a context, such as the *Jardin des Halles* in Paris, on a weekday afternoon. This is a central square with many people crossing it, strolling around it, or sitting on benches or on the ground. This situation can be associated with an *absolute legitimation*, which means nothing other than the absence of relative legitimation. Anyone is free to be there without being subject to any authorization and, in order to modify this equilibrium, the external world (the "other," the authorities, etc.) must propose that things be otherwise and justify its proposal. Such a justification may be based on more or less obvious reasons (someone walks around brandishing a machine-gun or lets her dog relieve itself against benches where other users want to sit and relax), but it always stems from the "intervening" party and not the user. In this type of situation, it is not the actor but the bearer of some institutional authority who queries the legitimacy of the use and undertakes the proof of *de*legitimation. Moreover, the question does not arise at any moment for the actor: there is no manifestation of prior control or surveillance of her action, which means that she does not perceive her own presence as an authorized behaviour.

2) Next, let us take a spatial context comparable to that of a kiosk in a public area (sidewalk, square, etc.). There is no limit (or perhaps not yet), no line that precisely delimits the surface on which the presence of an individual constitutes the proof or certainty of his status as a customer (although it is worth noting

---

13   On the unrecognized use of such simulations, see Gross and Rayner (1985).

that kiosks in Paris increasingly resemble "shops" with a clearly defined internal area). One can then ask: at what distance is one subject to the seller's interrogation? The seller will not question the passer-by if he looks at the newspapers without choosing, but will do so if the inspection exceeds a certain time, which varies according to the local norms (Paris differs from Marseille and Marseille from Algiers, etc.). In a word, one is legitimated to behave in different ways, arising from multiple choices that are subject to norms. One can associate this normativity with a *legitimation of public exchange.*

3) Then, let's take situations of "entry." Whatever the nature of the establishment, when one is inside, one is presumed to be seeking something that is linked to its function; entering a café automatically creates the supposition of something to do with "a café" and specifically "*this* café." So the question of legitimation does not arise in relation to the action of crossing the well-defined threshold, but it arises immediately when it comes to staying there. The multiplicity of options remains: one can sit down, wait for a friend who may not turn up, and leave without ordering if one does not feel embarrassed to do so. This is, however, the very opposite of absolute legitimation, since we must justify our presence but not our entry. We are in conditions of *self-declared legitimation.*

I do not claim that these three stereotypes reflect the multiplicity of manifestations of legitimacy, even in everyday experience; to show the multiplicity of such distinctions, one could refer to supermarkets, footpaths, public buildings, office buildings, and so on. But, what is useful to underline is the graduated character of the sphere of legitimacy and the element of *negotiability* within all these gradations. By this, I mean the set of socio-cognitive practices that touch on the possibility of linking the legitimate to the social. Negotiating thus implies the defence of interests perceived within the limits of options offered by the macro- and microsocial organization, i.e. mobilizing one's discursive and identity resources with maximum efficacy to justify one's position when this is subjected to questioning. In other words, it involves the practice and, therefore, reproduction of a culture: as Mary Douglas (1978: 6) puts it: "In his very negotiating activity, each is forcing culture down the throats of his fellow men. When individuals transact, their medium of exchange is in units of culture."

Negotiation thus remains the common element of all types of legitimation on condition that the questioner and the questioned have mutually intelligible social and cultural references. The point of arrival of this syllogism is the suggestion that all manifestations of the social that construct a self for others take part in this negotiating communication and are thereby integrated into the basis of the legitimation of an action. Everything that makes up identity and its constituent features – income, gender, colour, self-presentation, beauty, education, occupation, micro-culture, or attitude – in short, every socially assessable parameter, is constantly associated with the practices of negotiation and consequently reshaped. So what is the scope of functionality of the legitimate as a factor of the social operating via negotiation? The first dimension is that of self-proliferation. Negotiation sharpens skills and competencies that lead to the emergence of a self-identity and the management of the conditions that surround it. These skills lead in turn to an ever-greater negotiating competence.[14] In other words, the aptitude for negotiation as a part of interaction in society requires and generates a profound socialization. It goes without saying that this precise facet of socialization touches on the community dynamics of a society and counteracts any tendency toward isolation. The articulation of the link between the legitimate and the social is also expressed in a second important function of the negotiable, that of contributing decisively to the constitution of the symbolism of freedom. This function relies on a perspective that conceives the libertarian imaginary as a product of superimposed differentiations made on the basis of the distinction between the desirable and the permitted, a distinction that strongly depends on what is perceived as a legitimate action project in relation to the social affiliations of the actor. In fact, the negotiability of the social environment cements the intersection between the liberal consciousness and the consciousness that leads to the need for and the production of rules, the "nomogenic" consciousness. The silent integration of rules into the sphere of individual action, to which all reasoning immersed in social participation leads, is from this point of view only a secondary effect of practices of social negotiation. In its most important manifestations, socio-cognitive negotiability proves to be both a general factor of socialization and (re)production of identities, and a cognitive foundation of the conception and interrelation of two primordial poles of the political: freedom and the rule. In short, it would be hard to exaggerate the importance of a negotiable environment for any form of social organization developed up to our time.

---

14 Windish (1990: 212) notes that, contrary to what is often supposed in social psychology, "the subject does not only follow rules or laws, since in talking about the social, arguing about it, he creates, invents and reconstructs the social."

II.2 Reproduction of the Socio-cognitive

The substitution of binary alternatives for multiple forms of legitimation transforms the context of action in society into a series of prefabricated, non-negotiable options. If fundamental parts of the socio-cognitive, such as the communicative, the imaginary, and the nomogenic are subject to a rigid limit that splits the justification of the action in two, it is important to know the extent of this gap, why it is constructed, its direction, and its dynamics.

The first equation put forward (presence = legitimated presence) necessarily refers to automation. It seems fairly clear that the lack of leeway for modifying the context of action by communicative means (what I have called "negotiation'), the definitive aspect of the limit and especially the "technicity" of its realization establish that this is a process of labelling rather than of defining social status. What is the key element in this one-dimensional organization? If one simply answered: "the electronic dimension of the device," one would no doubt be on the right track. But (at the risk of tautology) a machine is only designed to perform repetitive tasks; an intelligent machine, such as a computer, has no other *raison d'être* than to calculate everything that is asked of it on a binary scale. Automation then consists in the realization of these two functions of the machine in everyday practice. The novelty, at least as regards sociological considerations, lies elsewhere.[15]

The inquiry performed by the control process addresses, in principle, the individual or "actor" who seeks entry to the closed space. In administrative language, this criterion would be expressed by the distinction between "holders" and "non-holders" of a valid ticket. However,

---

15 The implication is that sociological questions are here addressed only at the level of legitimation, negotiability and more generally the socio-cognitive. However, several kinds of impact on society emerge as consequences of information technology. For an overview, see Angell (1993).

such an approach masks the true content, and thereby the true consequences of non-negotiable legitimation. It would, by contrast, be more interesting to reflect on the reduction of all questions regarding the individual right of access to six centimetres of magnetic strip. This reduction introduces a new principle of correspondence between use and user into the functioning of the system: it is not Mr. or Ms. X who is granted the right to go through, but an indifferent individual possessing a code that the system recognizes and does not reject, by assigning to him or her the characteristic of "admissible." The core of this "admissibility" is transferred from the person to the code and translated from a natural language, a language of communication, into a technical language consisting only of affirmations and negations. The automaticity thus owes its existence to the re-encoding, which is the origin of its development. In the various facets of the procedure, one can identify the virtues that have led to its implementation: speed of selection; reduction of wage costs and lower commitment of human resources (employment being in the long run not only more expensive but also, above all, less reliable and controllable than mechanization); elimination of "leakage" through non-paying users in the network. The very logic of the device is rooted in the principle for which the user "practices" it, so to speak, since in social interaction between individuals the repetition of a behaviour acquires an inherent nomogenic capacity based on the presumption of the implicit consent of those who would be expected to react. This process is inconceivable in relation to the machine, onto which no consent can be projected.

In a sense, the place that my third proposition (selection = encrypted compatibility) occupies in this analysis is already circumscribed by the mutations bearing on the displacement of the legitimate from the communicative to the binary-alternative; but these mutations correspond to socio-cognitive transformations that are just as important.

When one speaks of "legitimation," one often means different things in terms of the scale that is intended. The content that Habermas (1976) attributes to the concept would be a good example of a large-scale approach, addressing the whole semantic field of the term. That is not the approach here. I do not even use Giddens's narrower definition, in which the individual remains the protagonist, albeit a collective individual, a symbol that facilitates the work of the author (Wacquant 1992). Furthermore, I do not mean political legitimation, the deficit of which was first exposed by Weber, although a legitimation deficit is always implied in my argument. Here, I concentrate on the legitimation of individual or atomized action, i.e. action individualized by external intervention. It should also be made clear that legitimation is not understood here as a sociologist's conclusion, but as the concrete situation in which the actor has the (unconscious) freedom; -the (conscious) right; -the permission (option); -or the authorization (a specific mandate) to perform an action or a series of actions.

I have already suggested that, at least as regards access to a closed environment, the legitimate is equivalent to the "compatible." It can be argued that this is more generally so, owing to the fact that each justification is a reference to a source of cognition acquiring a supra-personal power, either through the attribution of a community-wide consensus, or through a discursive or argumentative superiority. This super-session of the questioner and the questioned by the creation of an external, third-party ethos constitutes the birth of justice, of right (in the sense of "having the right to...") and of justificatory reason. It thus grounds the sociopolitical postulate that there are other limits to human action than power. The legitimate is an equilibrium of values that the actor judges accept-able (for himself and others) in the context of his action. This leads one to think that at least two types of consequences are necessarily attached to it: (a) a preliminary estimation of the limits of the negotiable, i.e. a constant tracking of the social envi-ronment, which represents an important effect at the level of social integration;[16] and (b) a reshaping of values through constant negotiation. Testing the limits and throwing a large measure of power into the balance are two of the most widespread tactics that lead to this renewal of the cultural through the legitimate.[17]

II.3 Binary Language

What then is the compatibility to which the response is a legitimate entry into the subway? The questioning that the system projects on us materializes in the repre-sentation of the user by a codified message; the device only speaks a binary language, and this is the language

---

16   An exemplary application of this function can often be seen in the behav-iour of parents: even if they think they "would be right" to admonish their child, they only do so in private.

17   The model conditions would be respectively the wretched stereotype of the would-be seducer who edges ever closer to the girl on the sofa, and the fact that "the client and the boss are always right."

one must simulate if one wants to get answers.[18] This language is not based on a will to control; quite the contrary, it embodies the ineluctable necessity of its own structuring. The device does not choose to select us as bringers of a message. *It can only impose this association* as a pre-condition of its own existence.

What is possible in this exchange is what can be translated in both directions. It is the user who is dependent on the feasibility and accuracy of this translation and not the reverse. This means that (a) the questioned actor is dependent on a language that, far from mastering, he does not understand, and (b) he is subjected to comparison with a series of predetermined options. The field of possible outcomes of this operation is not particularly broad. It is known to the point of self-evidence that two reactions can follow the insertion of a ticket into the slot of a turnstile: "Take back your ticket" or "Ticket invalid"; all contact with the system can only lead to one of these two options. These two points of arrival are the centres of convergence of all relations between the access control device and its environment. Any stimulus aimed at activating the device must belong to the foreseen probabilities, following the language of bits and bytes and the modular articulation of the system. The diagram below shows a simplified grid of the preconceived eventualities, taking the case of a user who tries to go through the turnstiles at Les Halles station and whose ticket corresponds to the cases in bold characters.

---

18 The examination of the language of the system is based here on its "quasi-social" behaviour, i.e. on its signifying reactions in a context of social interaction, since the device interests us here as a mediator of action, and not technically. This approach thus sets aside the stage of magnetic reading, which remains as a residue of analog (non-binary) technology, but which is then translated into digital language.

k_1	Place: Les Halles (Turnstiles between regional express network and urban subway)	
k_2	Zone:1	
k_3	Time now: 12:12:55	
	A	B
v_1	**Ticket for zones 1/2**	Ticket for zones 3/4/5, etc.
v_2	**No turnstile crossed in last 20 minutes**	Turnstile crossed in last twenty minutes
v_3	**No exit recorded**	Exit already recorded
v_4	Time now minus entry time ≤ 2hrs (less than 2 hours in network)	**Time now minus entry time > 2hrs (more than 2 hours in network)**
	↓	↓
	Access permitted (valid)	**Access denied (invalid)**

There are three constants, four variables, and two series of eventualities. The external world is reduced to the only three factors that "interest" the network, namely a space and time specific to its operation (k_1, k_3) and an organizational category (k_2). By contrast, the four variables refer to the internal evaluation the network makes and reveal the role of constants that relate exclusively to a representation of the social and natural world that enables the requested evaluation to be made. Time is represented *because* the system must not permit more than two hours' use with the same ticket (v_4) and must prevent reuse of the ticket (v_2); likewise, space is present only as "zone" or "exit," etc. This specific reflection of the world external to the system is subjected to four criteria set in a hierarchical structure as a binary scale of alternatives through the affirmative/negative outcome of each criterion. The grid thus expresses the fact that in order for the answer to be A, eventuality A has to be obtained for each criterion. If $v_1 + v_2 + v_3 + v_4 \ldots + v_n$ *and* $v_{1A} + v_{2A} + v_{3A} + v_{4A} \ldots + v_{nA}$, then A. Seen negatively, for any B in any position in the grid, the final answer is B. If, for example, the ticket "bears" a network entry time that is more than two hours old (v_{4B}), access will be denied.

This binary organization is integral to the way the computer has been designed to work. For everything that touches on the social, the program can be compared to such a grid of predetermined probabilities. Within its limits, no space can remain empty (a "bug" being just such a gap in foresight) since every possible stimulus must correspond in advance to a preconceived response. Every A or B, every "yes" or "no," condenses an archipelago of foreseen probabilities that lead to a certain response. One could, therefore, legitimately wonder: what place is there for a message unknown within this language? Could one hope to reduce one's travel budget by putting the ticket under the head of a tape recorder and recording the latest hit? There are serious reasons to assume that this will not work. More precisely, everything that is readable but unknown occupies a single place in the system regardless of its qualities, since one of the design objectives is indeed to eliminate doubt as such. The system automatically assigns a negative quality to any element alien to the reduction of the environment to a certain number of parameters. It makes the unknown recognizable by means of a blanket classification: every non-Yes and every non-No is equivalent to a No. To put it more informally, in the context of binary language, there is only one acceptable part of experience and everything that does not belong to it belongs to its opposite. To the disappointment of inventive travellers, it will not be a "Don't know" message that lights up at the turnstile, but "Ticket invalid."

II.4 Rigidity and Inversion of the Legitimate

The main conclusion to be drawn from the articulation of this logic is that it would be wrong to see the system as no more than a control mechanism, since it monitors neither an intentional behaviour nor even a key activity. On the contrary, it predetermines a field within which an activity can take place. It draws the boundaries of the realm of the possible. Outside those boundaries, there is no reference to any meaning. To spell out this supposition concretely in the practical context that concerns us, we must fill in the interstices of an ideal-typical approach by referring to the element that differentiates the simulation of the social universe from this domain, namely the emergence of the conditions that produce exceptions to the rules of the preconceived.

Ekeland quotes this tale from the Icelandic writer Snorri Sturluson and sees it as paradigmatic for probability theory and game theory:

There was a settlement on the island of Hísing which had alternately belonged to Norway and to Gautland. So the kings agreed between them to draw lots and throw dice for this possession. And he was to have it who threw the highest. Then the Swedish king threw two sixes and said it was no use for King Olaf [of Norway] to throw. He replied, while shaking the dice in his hand, 'There are two sixes still on the dice, and it is a trifling matter for God, my Lord, to have them turn up.' Thereupon he cast the dice, and one six showed up on one of them, but the other split in two, so that six and one turned up; and so he took possession of the settlement (Ekeland 1993: 3).

I shall present some less unlikely eventualities for my purposes. It is not hard to envisage situations that call into question the operation of a binary system, such as the following: you have just entered a station, but then realize that you do not have the details of your destination. You go out again to make a phone call; now you want to get back in.

Because one buys and uses a ticket as the token of obtaining a service, one would expect to be able to use the network. In a context of sociocultural justification (which the legal argument also follows), clearly what has happened is totally normal. Moreover, whether one takes one train or the next is all the same for the company that runs the network. However, the device rejects the use of the same ticket. It is a situation not foreseen by the system and, to bring us closer to the technical aspect, one that was never supposed to be foreseen; in practice, this indicates that it was never supposed to be treated as "having happened." The system does not adapt to the circumstances, but it mutates them to make them compatible with the preconceived options. Although it does not seem necessary, a configuration of the external world is integrated into the crossing of the threshold between the world of the self and the world of the network. Different rules, therefore, apply within the network, a fact that gives rise to the awareness of a not easily reversible move into an environment that has a different ethos of action, although the same actors take part in it. A fundamental difference is that the roles of the permitted and the forbidden are inverted as regards their relationship to the legitimate act: what is not explicitly permitted is forbidden, and not the reverse.[19] Reducing the social universe to a set of rules does not necessarily mean controlling it. The production of control refers to the independence of action, even potential independence; the surveillance that follows concentrates on the infinite manifestations of this poten-

19 This reversal recalls the practices of incarceration. Jacobs (1978) mentions the case of a prison governor who decided what items were contraband in his prison by listing all permitted items – all others were contraband.

tial for autonomy that only materializes in the event of
non-compliance with the projected norm. By reversing
this balance through the negation of what is permitted,
one also reshapes the relationship between action and its
cognitive and social origin. While the aim of an act is not
wiped out, the critical link between the act and its aim,
between *praxis* and *telos*, is broken by attacking the foundation of the processes that make the experiential world
graspable and intelligible.

The system does indeed have no space to accommo-
date that which is not previously envisaged – but why is
that? Clearly, the translatable message, and only that, is
efficient. From this point of view, the problem would be
summed up in a modification of the infrastructure such
that one could insert into the grid as a "yes" or "no" the
situation: "went out again without travelling, must now
re-enter." Technically, a touch screen and a series of
menus would be sufficient. Rapid and effective software
could translate the request so that the machine would
"recharge" our ticket.

The incompatibility of such a development with the
communicative capacities of the network is found in the
shadow of the language used and not in technical considerations. The problem does not concern the shaping
of the question, but of the answer. What the electronic
enzymes cannot digest is not our story but the fact that
we claim *it* happened to *us*. In other words, any envisageable reaction would have to include a judgement, an
evaluation of the situation based on direct references to
the social. If our request is to be granted, our individual
relation to what we claim has to be assessed. Everything
from the coherence of our story to our way of dressing
would play a role in such an assessment if it were made
without technical mediation. The likelihood is that we

would be believed, since it is a matter of belief, if we seem too wealthy to need to lie for a few francs, but our chances decline dangerously if the inspector is a member of a leftist organization. In short, everyday recourse to judgement inevitably consists in passing an examination in the ethos of public exchanges and the dominant values, or in Simmelian terms: "Even though our life seems to be determined by the mechanism and objectivity of things, we cannot in fact take any step or conceive any thought without endowing the objects with values that direct our activities" (Simmel 2004: 84).

This is the knot that a regularizing system cannot untie, and not only for reasons of technological capacity. An information environment that simulates human experience, known as "virtual reality," that can recognize everything the socialized individual can recognize, would automatically require that its operation be as hesitant as human action; that would be akin to the absurd idea of producing a map on the scale of what it represents.

II.5 Communicative Breakdown: the Incomprehensible

> *The mediation of meaning, as opposed to a system of given relations between things or processes, thus has an objective existence [...] as a particular activity (linguistic activity in the strict sense) governed by specific 'rules' [and] as an objectivation of the social structure in the process of reproduction (Freitag 1986: 81).*

One of the greatest secrets of the regularizing device is the dissociation that it introduces between the legitimating order and the socio-cognitive order. This dissociation takes place in the series of dichotomies that I have been

pointing to: judgement/value, knowledge/ethics, deci-
sion/freedom, *praxis/telos*, rule/reason. We are faced with
an unprecedented attempt at normalization of behaviour;
no reason relating to control, not even coercion, is given
to us for that normalization. What is more, the attempt
seems successful because we are not aware of it.

It is comfortable to examine the questions of control
and normativity in the exclusive context of domination
and then to resort to quasi-conspiracist analyses of the
social universe. However, it is difficult to reflect today on
the developments of the micro-social level as intentional
consequences of a project of domination. On the other
hand, since Foucault, it has become clear that one should
not necessarily attribute to the conditions of domination
a will that produces it, but should also regard the conditioning of the actors as the origin of these conditions.
Clearly, the subway turnstiles are not there to rob the
user of his socio-cognitive capital. A long series of reasons
that include cost limitation, increased revenue, improved
management, or the commitment to reducing "field
staff" are probably better explanations. That being so, we
clearly lack a hypothesis to analyze the consequences of
the device without attributing them to a will to dominate
emanating from some source. This hypothesis would have
to be oriented toward the communicative dimension of the
structure, because this is the only category that refers glob-
ally as an explanation to the actor's relation to the device
and the invisible absorption of all resistance within this
relationship. Therefore, the theorem to be demonstrated
is that, in the ambiguous conditions of the dispersion of
domination, what looks like an unconscious submission,
and is in any case a latent compliance, arises as the product

of a hegemonic model of communication.[20] In a sense, this suggestion includes a silent "updating" of the explanatory power of concepts such as hegemony or reification,[21] since it touches on the internalization of organizational priorities in the conditions of contemporary industrial societies.

As one passes through the device, the communicative neutralizes the conscious, i.e. frees the regularizing device from the obligation to attribute a socially meaningful symbolization for the actors. One of the many novelties of the system is the fact that the crucial language of the interaction is unknown to the user. I call this language crucial because it is precisely this coded language on which the decision is based and not on the natural language (e.g. French) that links the actor to the realization of his act. This coded language thus becomes the exclusive vehicle of power during the interaction between the user and the device, reducing any other communication structure to a simple means of internalizing the device's rigid and unalterable rules. As previously noted, the articulation of the process only authorizes a finite, definite series of messages oriented *toward* the network. In other words, there is a foreseen fixed number of propositions "intelligible" to the network, whose electronic transparency automatically entails their opacity for the actor. The fact that this coded language is not translatable makes these messages incomprehensible for the individual since, faced with the turnstile, she only knows that it must let

20 Applying the concept of hegemony to communication seems possible from a perspective that understands late modernity as a social condition developed around and controlled through the socio-cognitive. The insistence of the Gramscian model on the formation of consent can thus be extended for the communicative as a continuation of the ideological.

21 Taking for granted the limits of a regularizing device no doubt arises from reification, since it is based on a perception of what belongs to the social universe almost as if it were part of the natural world.

her through "because" she has a valid ticket. It would be
wrong to suppose based on this causal relation that the
actor understands what happens.

To clarify this point, we can again resort to the unfore-
seen. Suppose the ticket that "should" give us access
disappoints us – what options do we have? First, we can
repeat our action in case a momentary problem has arisen
and confirm that what has already happened is indeed the
case. After the four-letter protest that often follows irrita-
tions of this sort, there are only two legal routes, either to
use a new ticket or resort to the service window that, with
luck, exists and is open. This inevitable reasoning proves
in itself that we are, in some sense, aware of our inability to
understand and apply the communicative parameters of
the system to our advantage. Does the encoded information not exist for someone who does not know the code? We
can transpose the question into terms of human interaction: if we find ourselves in the middle of a square in Hong
Kong with a group of people explaining to us in perfect
Cantonese how to get to the bus stop marked on our map,
this is clearly not the same as if no one were speaking to
us, and we had never tried to get an answer. We understand that we do not understand and, moreover, that we
do not understand something specific, namely the answer
to our question, which is the crucial element in advancing
our plan of action. The situation leads to two observations
on how what becomes comprehensible enters everyday
experience: (a) in Hong Kong, one is *supposed* to speak
Cantonese, a fact that makes us a lost outsider and is part
of the framework of the legitimation of action in everyday
life. A language is thus legitimate in a context because it is
meaningful for the parties engaged in the interaction and,
in these terms, what exists *legitimately* as incomprehensible
in one environment establishes its legitimacy because it is

comprehensible *elsewhere*. So in relation to the functioning of the device we see a breakdown of the self-evidence of everyday action, a hidden breakdown, as we have already seen; (b) The nature of this breakdown is totally reversed, creating a legitimacy vacuum. The encoded language of the device is not incomprehensible here because it is comprehensible elsewhere. The network has its own semantics and, at the same time, this semantics is only meaningful within the network. Externality as such is identified with exclusion. The system becomes a hermetic cell in the midst of the experiential world. However, its integration into this world is based on the fact that the absolute impenetrability of the language invented by its designers is accepted as such by the users, which confirms that there is no resistance to the operating principles of the device. The corollary would be that if this combined development is sufficiently widespread, we would perhaps here find ourselves at the start of the disappearance of the experiential world through the meshes of the actor's cognitive net.

II.6 A Hierarchy of Obstacles

The dysfunctions used so far to explore the minute social dynamics of a subway ticket have a point in common: the compliance of the actor's behaviour with the limitations of the regulating process. Suppose that after going out to make that phone call, we are sufficiently agile to get through the turnstile without a ticket. Suppose too that a plain-clothes inspector sees us doing so. He asks us to pay the prescribed fine or, if we cannot, to produce ID in exchange for a ticket with which we can proceed on our journey. According to the rules, we have committed an offence and, moreover, at the wrong time. What is our position? We entered "irregularly," and this is forbidden.

We already know why the regulation is established so as to recognize exclusively the existence of its own context and to ignore the practical reality; any other solution would annul the operating principle of the system. Everyone could claim that they had just gone out, had lost their ticket, did not know that they were in Zone 3, or had had an urgent need to visit the toilets before the end of their journey. This framework of suppositions shapes precisely the causal logic, according to which we must now hand over the sum requested. Moreover, we know that we entered illegally because the machine told us so.

Here is an ancient distinction: the one between the motive and the consequence of an action. Among other things, it is also the founding category of legal responsibility. Not surprisingly then, behind this punitive exchange lies a hierarchy of difficulties. If we decided to contest a fine in terms of what seems just, we would face a long legal process against an all-powerful adversary, an institution for which what is at stake is its sovereignty over the network. Even, in the unlikely event that we won the case, everything would soon be put back as it was by the new law that the Minister of Transport would promptly lay before Parliament. For, it is not the legal order that can abolish the operating principle of the established economic order, but only applications of political will or social dynamics capable of intervening at the heart of the demands of the economic structure. Pierre Legendre (1983: 17) extends this dependence of the legal to include its active contribution to maintaining the "dogmatic" truth of industrial spaces, observing that "legality functions not only to make things work, but as a discourse theatrically reproducing the truth." Integrated into such theatricality, the imaginary legal challenge I have suggested tends to show that a central element in the analysis of a regulating process is the structuring of an invisible hierarchy of hurdles as a basis for persuasion by deterrence, a mechanism that gives crucial but hidden support to the edifice of regularization.

II.7 The Socio-technical

The issue of challenging the system only arises in a legal context. In the framework of everyday practice, we know we need to have a valid ticket; this is part of the elementary skills of a city dweller. How do we learn that the validity of the ticket is a matter for the technical competence of the turnstiles and not our own individual judgement? Through the banality of the activity involved, through the secondary character of the acts that make up the relationship with the device. Every day, we put our ticket in the slot while looking at something else, thinking about our personal finances, or talking to a colleague. In short, we are doing everything except wondering whether we are inserting a valid ticket. The device transforms the question of value into skill in the coordination of movements, the cultural into the praxic. For the user, synchronization with the rhythm of the flow of which she is a part belongs among the mechanisms of social integration, as becomes apparent through the negative consequences that await actors who induce breakdowns or malfunctions into the system.[22] It is not a question here of confidence in expert systems but of an interactive, practical behaviour formation presented by the device to each user. The process *decides* on the unfolding of the user's actions and channels her behaviour based on tokens of legitimation that

---

22 Wendy Leeds-Hurwitz (1989: 110-18) distinguishes between two conditions (self-synchrony and interactional synchrony) and their breakdown (asynchrony or dyssynchrony). Manifestations of dyssynchrony attract the reproving attention of the other actors involved and the device. The dynamics of this situation lies at the centre of the universe of regularization.

she provides, or not. This interaction may be frequent
and repetitive and, as we have seen, it invisibly imposes
the preliminary acceptance of its uniform rhythm, its
impenetrable logic and final decision. In short, it does not
simply normalize behaviour; it assimilates it into an environment where it has no sense except as the object of the
process. We know that we are in an "irregular situation"
because we know the rule. "They" cannot know whether
we are right. But, "we" can, and we do; we also know that
being right will not help us. To speak of internalization
here, is an understatement. If we assume that the actor
silently accepts the rules or that the rules are integrated
into the actor's reasoning, this in no way reaches the full
the depth of the problem. More concretely, that would
be to forget the active participation of the individual in
this reasoning. In an article that reveals the unity of the
biological and the social, Grant Gillett shows that cognition as a neurobiological function is constantly reshaped
through social interaction and that understanding and
acting consist in learning rules through this interaction.
It is of course possible to ignore the rules but people
mostly follow them without deciding to obey them.
Gillett (1993: 39) thus poses the question of internalization in new terms: "What is more, we have noted that
in shaping her behaviour so that it realises the rule, the
subject takes normative attitudes to her own dispositions
and responses...."

The more one is subject to the modalities of a process,
the more one's adherence to the process is reinforced[23]
and, consequently, the more the modalities are perceived
as "natural," until they reach the point of total integration
into the representation of our social universe, i.e. the level

---

23   For an analysis of the mechanisms of "social corroboration," see
     Steinbruner (1974: 121ff).

of the cultural mediation of the self.[24] The main transformation to be observed in the light of this widening spiral is that, in a way not seen before, *behavioural compliance emerges as the product of an exchange within the self, an exchange that the mediation of the regularizing device merely triggers.*

II.8 Regularization: Human - Machine Interaction

Strictly speaking, the actor does not comply with norms – rules that come from a certain source and guide behaviour – but, in a paradoxical and new way, she complies with herself, the self of yesterday that dilates today to be superseded by that of tomorrow. The extent of the exercise is remarkable: the Paris Transit Authority (RATP) transports 1,221 million passengers a year, an average of 4 million a day (discounting holidays), including weekends.[25] This makes it probably a more common activity than buying a newspaper, shopping, or even going to work (students and school pupils, the unemployed and the retired all take the subway).

Beyond the question of the underlying obligation, it is also interesting to clarify the practical realization of the inspecting functions. It is possible for an inspection process to be entrusted to an electronic device, but can the function of a machine be defined as an act? In the sense that it relates to the unknown, the question is philosophical. However, it can be addressed here in its context of interaction in society. What makes the machine "act" 'is not its "machinality" but its "non-humanity." Its

---

24 In a way, Karl Mannheim's observation (1943: 23) that "every new system of social controls requires the re-education of the self" is here transposed into the context of human-machine interaction.

25 Data from 1990 for a population of 9,318,821 in the Paris conurbation (INSEE 1993: 18). In an advertisement, the RATP boasts that it can "transport half the planet each year and be interested in every one of [us]."

mediating dimension, its transfer of human will, and especially its response to human will – that of the user – is what makes its functioning an act. The reflection of a human dialogue on its screens, in an interpretable form, is socially significant precisely as communicative and more generally socio-cognitive event. The space of the inspection should be conceived in different terms, as functioning through effects on the action of the inter-locutor whom it inspects.

While the concept of inspection helps update our theorizing of control in the light of contemporary developments, it is clear that there are sub-sets within it. A clear division could, for example, be based on whether or not the machine is involved in the inspecting task. As regards the proposed criteria of specificity (lack of negotiability, incomprehensibility, self-mediation), it is clear that the act of inspection does not fulfil them entirely and constantly. Social life is not yet a vast network endlessly confronting us with limits that are both insurmountable and incomprehensible. However, the possibility of such a future should not be ruled out. On the contrary, the existing signs support rather than discredit that hypothesis.

The key element here is that the process mediates the representation of the world for the individual involved: an aspect of control is introduced into behaviour as such; the policing parameter is integrated into action itself, so that the action cannot be separated from this parameter without losing its meaning. Thus, turnstiles would have no sense if tickets were handed out free to everyone, or if they let everyone through, or if they sorted users on an abstract or totally unknown principle, etc. Unlike a generic inspection process, the regulating process is monolithic. An act of regularization cannot have any other meaning than to question and control, as is the case for other acts of inspection; the specific qualities of the regularizing device refer only to a techno-communicative level.

We now have to reorganize this material in terms of a purely sociological categorization. We already know that the main element in the impact on the targeted actor is the introduction of higher degrees of "normality" (in the sense of naturalness) in controlling his behaviour. From this standpoint, the regulating process operates as a mechanism diffusing a new culture of control. A second standpoint should address the importance of the machine for the specificity of the social consequences of the process. How does the machine become meaningful? Or, closer to the heart of the problem, how does the use of the machine alter the contact between the still-human questioned actor and the questioner, even if the latter articulates the message of the institution? Can the lack of comprehensibility, the automatic act, the translation to which the mediation of the machine subjects this relationship, be concentrated into a totality that is meaningful from the point of view of the consequences of the "third-party" role of the machine?

The crucial element in arriving at such a totality would be the absolute attachment of the machine to a group of predetermined criteria, excluding any other condition or any other reference to the external world. For example, the turnstile will not let people through more quickly if there is a fire in the station unless the system is specially programmed to detect the event and "react" in a certain way to messages from sensors. The second sociologically important dimension, which may be widely ignored because of its self-evidence, is the fact that the targeted population *recognizes* the system's inability to take account of parameters of action other

than those that interest the questioner. This acceptance, which automatically signals an internalization, as
I have already suggested, also constitutes the precondition for the processing of the individual by the device.
In other words, it is the reification of the priorities and
the monolithic mechanical, magnetic, electric or electronic dimension that make maximum internalization
possible. This reasoning – tautological or not – enables
us to reach two useful conclusions:

1. The important thing is the "mechanicity" of the
process in absolute terms, not its "machinality" as such.
For our analytical needs what is important is its autistic,
inflexible logic, closed to external influence. Now, if
instead of the automatic devices, there were human
beings who adhered in the same way to the predetermined
criteria of selection and set up a break in communication between themselves and the targeted population,
one would still have an act of regularization. I offer as
an example a hospital employee who, working behind a
thick glass screen, is supposed to direct women to Office 1
and men to Office 2. The legitimation of this action is no
different from a regularizing device. The person cannot
be subjected to a counter-questioning about the causes of
his action. "Why are men sent to Office 2?"; "Why are men
and women separated?" or "Can I go to the office for the
opposite sex?" are meaningless questions in the face of
such a process.

However, it is possible to envisage conditions in which
such questions are possible: coming from someone
who partially eludes the power of the norms (a child, a
madman, an inebriate, etc.), the inquiry is legitimated.
One can assume a reaction that may range from an understanding smile to a brusque rejection. But, in any case,
it will be a socialized reaction, drawn from a personal

resource that dissociates itself from the process and does not bear on its specific characteristics. What I wanted to demonstrate very briefly is that human involvement, subject to the social ethos, within a regulating system always has a potential to threaten the system, but one that can only reveal itself in extraordinary and, therefore, statistically marginal conditions. The importance of this potential is further diminished for two reasons. The first is the expansion of automation for all activities, a tendency more marked in the universe of control processes than in other areas. The second, given its "lower" efficiency and reliability, human involvement, when it exists, is reserved not for sorting but for the application of the consequences that automatic sorting entails. Very often, it is reserved for repressive or punitive measures that underlie the compliance with the selection that the process implements. Human intervention tends toward ensuring that the excluded cannot have access to what is only offered to those selected and that those who take the risk of defying this are punished. It is no accident that subway inspectors position themselves *behind* a set of turnstiles. Their work does not contradict the selection already made but reinforces it. One can be sure that the human link in the chain exists only where engineering cannot yet provide solutions, or at least not solutions as effective as, and less expensive than, human labour.

2. As a general effect of the rigidity of the device, its automatic interactivity, in fact, suppresses the "too slow" and "too ambiguous" communicative skills of the user. This enables us to see the mechanical aspect of a regulating act as a dimension reinforcing and consolidating the mediation that the process inculcates in the targeted individual.

II.9 Self-Mediation and the Horizon of the Possible

The mediating function concerns the capacity of the medium to fix a part of reality (whatever "reality" may mean) and launch it into an environment where it can have a use that benefits the receiver. The point of anchorage would be the detachment of a slice of a process and its diffusion to those who are interested in it, or, in a more developed stage, to those whom the sender wants to reach. Whether it be a drop of river water that finally comes out of the tap, the fraction of a worker's activity that corresponds to one dollar, or the image of a child killed by a shell on the other side of the world,[26] the medium provides the receiver with the product of a context whose processes of emergence are not present. In the case of the regulating process, it disembeds and petrifies the socio-cognitive context at the moment of contact with the device, which thus becomes the medium itself. This context is reactivated at the next contact, i.e. remains fixed in experience and resurfaces, reinforced and therefore more acute, at each passage. It is not simply a matter of people thinking less about what they do than in the past, but the introduction of a new order alien to and sealed off from the world of experience. At the moment of passage, the device invisibly injects the principles of its hermetic universe into everyday experience and so interposes itself between two conditions of interaction and two conditions of the processed actor. The process thus diffuses the experience of an encrypted, evasive universe and each time takes increasing possession of the sphere of the negotiable. In so doing, it also projects a new representation of the actor's relationship with his social environment, since it involves him in a radically new simulation of interaction.

---

26 It is possible to see in this suggestion the point of convergence between Georg Simmel's essay on money, the general theses of Marshall McLuhan and "mediacentric" work.

Clearly, in quantitative terms, the important element in this mediation lies in its identical repetition, which is the *raison d'être* of the machine. The difference between a regulating process and other forms of inspection, on the one hand, and between social control and normalization, on the other hand, is finally clarified and justified. The regularization of behaviour does not mean constraining it or limiting it to the fields prescribed by a source of decision or a planning centre, or even a sphere authorized by membership of a group or of society. Regularization is the effect of a mechanically repetitive process that relies on its neutrality, i.e. its attachment to a legally and socially hegemonic goal (for example, preventing non-payment in the subway, theft of money from automated teller machines (ATMs), or terrorist attacks in air planes with the aid of metal-detecting gateways, etc.) and the consequent creation of a clearly understood environment where the pursuit of this goal is more than inevitable: it is natural. Thus, repetition itself suffices for people not to think that we perhaps need a subway without turnstiles. The regularizing impact is far more effective than any other form of control even if it is less voluntary. The regulating process does not impose the choice of one alternative among others; it suppresses the emergence of alternatives by creating a clear and predictable world that refers only to the regular rhythm and the coordination of the acts that compose it. That is why imposing a routine behaviour that follows the rhythm given by the device helps to unravel the skein of mass society; to regularize is not to control, it is to shape a controlled subject or, more precisely, an actor who can only act in a way compatible with the process. As a result, regularization erodes the link between the level of interaction and the level of social organization by setting up a consciousness that takes for granted what it experiences and no longer

has the means of attaining another level of comprehending
the social. Therefore, the problem arises not in terms of
the inability to contest a given structure but the inability to
envisage the social world in critical terms.

The question becomes even more complex when
considered in the light of the problematic of repression.
One can combine the extent of alternative visions of the
social with the possibility of grasping the present as the
bearer of some kind of oppression. It is, so to speak, as
much in spite of as because of the oppressing tendencies that the demand for autonomy can arise. However,
in the procedural reality of regularization, the notion
of resistance finds no foothold, no *raison d'être*. Because
the effect of the device remains below the surface
and its language encrypted, its effects are not readily
apparent to its user. It should not, however, be taken
for granted that this invisibility is set in the unconscious
and so remains excluded from the political, i.e. unable
to produce tangible results. Marianne Gullestad (1992:
38) suggests a shift in analytical approach to grasp this
political content of the everyday:

"[...] instead of distinguishing between conscious practices or aspects of practices (ideology) and unconscious
ones (mentality), I suggest that we distinguish between
explicit ideas open to debate and the implicit frameworks
of meaning within which such debates are meaningful.
Such implicit frameworks of meaning are generally taken
for granted and seldom liable to open discussion".

Although it refers to interpersonal interaction, this
proposition is even more valid for relations with an automated actor; because the fact that the reactions of the
machine are by definition unopposed is only the symptom
of a taken-for-granted cognitive framework that makes any
act of resistance meaningless.

At present, it is impossible to answer the central question that these conditions raise, namely, whether we have come to the end of the long and powerful line of movements of massive oppositional action. It may be that we are talking here about the invisible foundations of a political late modernity that obeys dramatically different rules and that is establishing itself as a self-evident and inevitable paradigm of social coexistence organized around a consensus on the "third way." In any case, it seems that mutations of the socio-cognitive order define what is politically or otherwise possible, given that they operate at the level of the conceivable, of which the possible is only a part, and that any modification of the *status quo* bears on this distinction. If we identify the two, as regularization leads us to, we are not simply changing the perspective on the balance of the political dynamics of a society but abolishing even the existence of such a perspective. In other words, the political becomes a continuous space of competent, specialized management, in all cases external and with no relation to the individual except in order to apply this management. It is no coincidence that this description evokes both regularization and the phenomena of political disengagement and apathy.[27] It is, on the other hand, very probable that the self-evidence of everyday actions holds the key to links that remain so unnoticed and so important. I do not, of course, present this proposition as a conclusive affirmation but as a direction that research has not yet explored, no doubt because such an approach appears too banal and too microscopic to nurture the social production of the political.

---

27 Between 1962 and 1988, the percentage of manual workers in France who declared themselves "very" or "fairly" interested in politics fell by 22 points (Capdevielle, Meynaud and Mouriaux 1990: 37, 94ff).

II.10 Selective Access and Technocentric Equality

We have seen that the potential for identical repetition lies at the heart of the concept of regularization. This can be observed from the angle of its political dimension when it is juxtaposed with the fact that the identical treatment of actors by institutional or other authorities is a major political demand in a state subscribing to the "rule of law," or rather a state based on the principles of modernity and promoting modern visions as part of its projected image. I refer of course to the democratic, individualist, egalitarian model, which, at least as an imaginary authority, dominates post-industrial societies. Does a regulating process meet the specifications of these models and, if so, for which reasons? In the first instance, one can more easily affirm that this is the case by following the *via negativa*: the inherent machinality leads to the impossibility of discrimination. An Armani suit or a punk hairstyle will not influence the machine. Moreover, each actor takes for granted that it is so for everyone else, and assumes that others can only think the same way. This event passes unnoticed, but as soon as it emerges from the shadow of the habitual it has to be recognized as a historical novelty of the first degree. It can be argued that, without fireworks or fanfare, the social visions that inspired political movements, the struggles of centuries, the ideals for which as much ink as blood has flowed, in a word the egalitarian grand narratives, have now been realized in their pure, absolute and irreversible form in the subway station, the bank, and the airport. The equality realized through a metal box measuring 2m x 1m is not *a relative equality*, like that of "more equal" Orwellian pigs, but the indisputable, unequivocal equality of all towards all. Even the refinements of the discursive realization of domination are here eliminated by definition, because in the first place the machine is impervious to any external language; in fact, it lies outside the socio-cognitive as such in the ideal condition of pure judgement and asocial technodicy. It is clear that the social consequences implied are symptoms of the function of a system, depending on the efficacy of the machine in order to manage (i.e. allow the existence of) ever greater, faster, and more mobile flows. In an iconoclastic essay, Gellner (1987: 110) suggested that "arguments about equality, fairness and justice, which tend to take egalitarianism for granted and make few attempts to seek its social roots, seem to me doomed to a certain superficiality." Exploring that social depth, one can assert that, for the first time, we have reached a point where it would be impossible even to suspect that things are less than ideal at the level of the egalitarian treatment of citizens by institutions. Not only is the absolute envisageable, but also it becomes accessible to all and at all times.

I interrupt this eulogy to ask why such a development has not struck us. A plausible supposition would be that not every social mutation has to be an epic. However, it is more justifiable to think that, in late modernity in particular, important transformations take place in an imperceptible way that is integrated into the socio-cognition of the everyday. One would have to reconstitute the past with the aid of a history manual or an encyclopedia for women's suffrage or access to the labour market to move into the sphere of the new and extraordinary. In other words, the repetitive present can only be normal, natural, and banal. So the fact that we do not notice it does not mean a major mutation is not emerging and propagating itself.

Hence, if regularization also means equality, and even prototypical equality, there still remains a major consequence that we must consider – in particular, the fact that such a development is brought about by a control structure, another change for which it would be hard to find a precedent. There is thus a dimension that the advocates of equality should celebrate in the domain of inspection, and more precisely, of regularization: the advent of a social pedagogy that inculcates in everyone, regardless of class, age, status, or prestige, the sense of being treated in the same way and belonging to the same group defined by its common reference to the use of a service. Here, we see the image of a peaceful revolution that abolishes classes, achieving an exploit comparable to that of a fast-food restaurant where a young executive may stand in line between a homeless person and a school student.

If the monosemy of the world is the price to be paid for a "just" world, if we are equal because the only practised and imaginable world is a world of equals, from what angle should we consider this development: that of the desirable result or the restrictive principle? It is a question that will soon give political philosophy much food for thought. The socially practised dimensions of this development are, however, founding elements of a sociological examination of the link between control and distributive justice.

But, equality in what? From the moment that equality is diffused, so to speak, and not won or at least consciously asserted, the question of its meaning and its social differentiation arises. From the point of view of what Pierre Bourdieu calls "distinction," the regulatory effect proves neutralizing. Since the process does not recognize behaviours but identical positions, the targeted individual is deprived of a reasoning that is capable of supporting attempts at distinction. The uniform result guaranteed by machine treatment places any attempt by the individual to create a distance outside the social legitimacy of action practically in the psychopathological sphere. Thus, regularization constitutes an accepted singleness of purpose; it also colonizes the cultural fields of class identity or at least the membership of a more restricted total than the whole society; it modifies and reduces the possibility and scope of mechanisms devoted to reproducing the diversification of social statuses.[28] The rigidity of the regulating effects is also seen in the fact that they are products of the aggressiveness, or, to put it another way, of the initiative of the device, which acts without behavioural reactions being able to establish any reality in response to these effects. The progression of individual reality is not effected according to a deaf and blind model, but rather that of a "juggernaut"[29] in which one enters into a context of experience not only to follow a foreseen path, but also to hand oneself over to a pre-calculated sequence of emotions and sensations, in short, a complete and simplified experience whose only condition of existence is the immersion of the actor in the dynamics that produces it. As a consequence, and within the limits of what concerns us here, regularization introduces the construction of an equitable civic edifice independent of any discourse, any process, and even any political will. The mutations of the order concerned therefore imply that the current conceptualization of the political is mostly indifferent to a plethora of developments that could render it obsolete.

If one considers the question of the birth and the widespread development of an "involuntary" political sphere, one must also ask in relation to what this sphere is formed. Given that inequality and issues associated with it exist across different societies, including post-industrial societies, there is every interest in examining questions of equality from this angle. Up until now, one has always

---

28 John Shotter (1993: xi ff.) gives a striking account of the processes of differentiation in the framework of occupational coexistence and their serious consequences for the formation of self-identity. See also Sennett and Cobb (1972).

29 Giddens (1990: 139) presents this model as a symbol of late-modern experience.

been equal or unequal in relation to something. Is this still the case and, if so, what is this "something" around which regularity laboriously weaves its web of fairness?

First, it is access: the shift from the "open" world of absolute legitimation to the world of the admitted, of those who have a right to a space, a service, or something else for which the regulating process forms the threshold. However, the selection between the admitted and the excluded itself establishes a stratifying operation, in that it differentiates between the possessors of signs of access and the rest, thus placing itself at the heart of an inequitable distribution. Posing the question in a more general context, Miles (1988: 138) includes in his table of the "crucial issues of the information society" the theme of the restructuring of interests: "How far will new communities of interest emerge spontaneously from the public and how far will they be the product of organizations with the financial power and professional skill to define and package issues in particular ways?" In a similar vein, Fréchet (1993) analyzes the formation of increasingly fragmented "clienteles" as a symptom of the information technologies. He concludes that the management of stratifying priorities by the services offered to these clienteles seems to be becoming increasingly complicated, to the point of splitting the individual into segments belonging to the different identities assigned by the state and other institutions.

II.11 Desocialized Selection

In a regulating context, there is always a link between all the actors concerned – the selection itself, their questioning by the process – which means that the target population in fact comprises both the admitted and the excluded insofar as they are potentially "admissible." We thus return to the more general problematic of the control of behaviour.

The only *raison d'être* not only of regularization, but also of any act of inspection, is the possibility of non-compliance with the essential rules of the activity that this act covers. All inspection is oriented not toward compliance but non-compliance, in the sense that it does not seek to ensure that compliance is present but that deviance is absent. The attitude that examines – or rather conceives the ambition of examining – normality as a facet of reality as plausible as non-normality is a critical, i.e. scientific, attitude. Outside of the scientific approach, in the social world, the normal is not an observable space, but only experienced and received as "natural." It is the exceptions, the instants and manifestations that do not find their place in it, that make the normal what it is only very exceptionally supposed to be: perceptible. As a consequence, a process of normalization does not generally demand compliance with rules that are consciously followed, but contravenes the negation of continuation, the break with what constitutes a rule only by its established existence.

In these circumstances, any attempt at inspection should be understood as a detection not of the normal but of its absence. By contrast, a regulating process diffuses an artificial awareness of normality in that it constantly and minutely verifies its existence. The collective socio-cognitive foundation that takes certain conditions of the social for granted is thus drained into a reflexive consciousness that apprehends each eventuality as a probability amenable to technical processing rather than as an act that is observable only when it is deviant. By bringing together the normal and the deviant to face the same technical questionning, the regulating process takes away the sense of the norms and values that underlie it. The regulating process has no benchmarks to evaluate socialized human behaviours, and no channel to communicate the information essential for designating the limits and intentions of these behaviours. The fact that the "theatre of everyday life," as Erving Goffman (1969) famously described it, forms the basis of an infinite series of distribution of social statuses is too self-evident to be surprising. But, the depth of this process contains precise hypotheses with concrete consequences. For our purpose, the distinction between persons or situations according to their perceived social "aptitude" is also made on such a basis. I cannot resist quoting a passage from *The Homeless Mind*:

> Suppose you are waiting in an airport lounge prior to going on a plane trip and you see the pilots walking toward the plane across the tarmac – two stereotyped counter-cultural types, with shaggy hair and beads, moving loose-limbed to an unheard rock rhythm, one of them [...] puffing on a marijuana joint. Would you take a trip on this plane? The answer, we believe, is obvious – no matter how great your sympathies with the counterculture (Berger, Berger and Kellner 1974: 193-4).

The archipelago of socially significant signs (gestures, expressions, voices, clothes, etc.) that the individual establishes as an object of socialization is ordered and classified in a concrete ethos and finally situated in relation to the dominant axes of values. The attribution of assumptions concerning the observer's interests forms the core of this evaluation. Goffman (1971) speaks of practices of "civil inattention" when analyzing the ways in which we reassure others and persuade ourselves that others do not threaten us. However, these practices, which give the feeling of guaranteed security, are profoundly dependent on the evaluation of the "normality" of others, i.e. an evaluation that implies that their behaviour will proceed as we think it "should," and that works on a host of cues from which we extract an overall message at a glance. The relationship between this message and the order of social stratification is very close, and the hypothesis that the former is only the imprint of the latter in the cognitive mechanisms of each actor is not easy to discredit. This correspondence, although both reinforcing social division into classes and being based upon it, does not aim to produce these consequences. We do not take account of social stratification *because* we have the intention of reproducing it, but because we think that the social signals that the individual concerned transmits constitute an often very reliable guide to his behaviour toward us. This may be a circle of self-evidence, but it hardly reduces the validity of the outcomes that are thus produced.[30]

II.12 Equality in Suspicion: the Demise of "Decent People"

To take effects for causes is the everyday basis of social division. For example, we rely on the supposition that a man wearing an expensive suit, with a leather briefcase in his hand and the *Financial Times* under his arm, is not going to snatch our handbag, any more than the lady seen rushing to the supermarket dragging her child along with her, or the gentleman walking his daughter to school. Clearly, we feel able to define certain categories of persons as "decent." Those who are strangers to us but do not seem to be bearers of an interest

---

30 Anatole France (1987: 399) sardonically described the injustice of a judgement that always lands on its feet when he wrote of "the majestic equality of the law, which forbids the rich as well as the poor to sleep under bridges, to beg in the streets, and to steal bread."

running counter to our image of society are counted among the "decent people," also known as "respectable, law-abiding citizens," or "honest folks." By this, we mean "people like us," people who are "normal," or "cool," who have "class," or "principles," who are "well educated," "well brought up," "respectable," "poor but honest," or "God-fearing," depending on the observer's particular slant. In other words, for the majority of us, the majority of individuals are "decent." Thus, as well as being an efficient means of producing stratifying representations, personal social typology also provides a platform for the generation of presumptions about the "decency" of the majority of individuals in relation to most of their actions. It is important to stress the notion of "decency" and its social positivity, which is granted selectively in the interaction between strangers. In society, one must prove one's innocence by one's presence, in contrast to law, where the legal presumption of innocence, reiterated by modernity and applied by capitalist democracies,[31] seeks precisely to limit the excesses of intuitive social judgement. This legal presumption, in fact, represents the need to question ourselves regarding the compatibility of the person's intentions and actions with the demands of the normative or legal order. Thus, it realizes a right of the citizen vis-à-vis the institutions, an equilibrium generated and applied by the law. The person who benefits from this model is already under examination. By contrast, "decent," "law-abiding" citizens are those who do not need this type of protection and who, in everyday exchanges, would not come under any suspicion, a condition which now changes as soon as they confront a regularizing device.

---

31   In practice this is the legal principle that is made concrete in the presumption of penal law *in dubio pro reo* – "when in doubt, for the accused."

In terms of social control, the '"decent citizen" represents the constant nurturing of a hegemonic core of behaviours that reiterate the forms and rules to be followed in social coexistence.

The necessary grounding of the status of the "decent citizen" on communicating socially recognizable signals means automatically that it is impossible for the regulating environment to grant such a status, owing to the hermetic character of its mechanical order. This allows us to conclude with certainty that regularization remains both: (a) a means that antagonizes the reproduction and renewal of the communicative and cultural conduits of social stratification, and (b) a vehicle for the suppression of socio-cognitive functions that generate and perpetuate the collective representation of an *a priori* law-abiding society. Regularization is thereby a factor of elimination of the functional consequences of this model of representation at all three levels of the individual social ethos, socialization and the social organization itself. The hypothesis then leads to the emergence of another type of society as regards the projections of its own normality, of which it makes use in multiple ways.

Moreover, the equity that a regulating process sets up among its targets can now be clarified in its two facets. First, it concerns an obligation and not a right: the obligation imposed on everyone to be subject to a decision on a single criterion that is objective and identical for everyone and perceived as such by everyone. This decision concerns an "a-individual" quality projected onto the individual: the possession of a token for access. The second facet concerned by this development informs us about what the process imposes as a precondition for its decision. In contrast to a communicative interaction, we see here the prior, uniform, compulsory attribution of a presumption of guilt.[32] Reproduced at its mechanical rhythm, the regulating environment questions its targets on the only hypothesis possible for its structure, that of the identical probability of non-compliance for each actor, without exception. It becomes the point of convergence, the only site of communication of the targeted individuals, who can aspire to the status of law-abiding citizen only after, and with the aid of, the regulating decision. The attribution of legitimacy is now reduced to the order of the effect of a decision lacking social foundation. Moreover, the erosion of this category is not replaced or substituted by another socially produced legitimacy, but creates a vacuum by assigning it to the realm of the unintelligible. The demise of "decent, law-abiding citizens" and their replacement by "potential offenders" would be less important without the dynamics of isolation that accompanies it. It would hardly be justified to ignore the fact that "decent citizens" constitute a set to which the individual is admitted through social representations. Membership of this imaginary set produces multiple motivations linked to the actor's attachment to his society since he necessarily defends the representation of his own self through the obligatory mediation of his memberships and loyalties. Being this or that could be seen as the certificate of the existence of a self that self-refers and self-identifies in relation to its social context, and symmetrically, of a society whose public sphere cannot make itself immune to developments regarding individual projections of

---

32 Gary Marx (1988: 149) rightly sees in this facet a means of control, the pervasion of the wider society by applications previously reserved for the penal environment. However, it is important to conceive this development not as voluntary but as *necessary* in order to understand and evaluate it.

social membership. More concretely, such an intertwining of the individual with the social counters any tendency toward exclusion, if by that is meant not a highly unequal access to consumption, but the development of a distance that places the individual outside his own representation of society, a distance which makes him a unit that is no longer socialized.

II.13 Atomization

By affecting the link between the modes of traditional communicative legitimacy and the non-emergence of excluding tendencies, the regulating process favours the production of vacuums oriented toward the establishment of a society with a privileged core and a periphery of isolated fragments. But, aside from its excluding effects, regularization sets up a specific model of isolation, since the identification or substitution of the individual by the possession of a token of access presupposes the atomization of the targeted population.

Every route toward the grouping of actors or toward the existence of an actor's recourse to others is definitively closed. The regulating environment has no means of representing the links between its users. Each user thus finds herself alone before the process, conscious of the fact that any relationship bearing on her practical or imaginary contact with others cannot be translated into machine language. The positively atomizing character of the process through the banishment of all intersubjectivity from its universe eliminates in the actor even the motive for claiming membership of a larger context. So the device acts at two levels to produce isolation and, thereby, exclusion: first, by dismantling the structures that relied on a communicative control, which regularization replaces, and which reproduced and reconfirmed

the actor's links with her society; and second, by eliminating the *raison d'être* of the references to the social
that the individual would have made under the pressure
of now non-existent motives. The regulating process is
thus highly charged with a dimension of *desocialization*
conveyed by the egalitarian distribution of potential guilt
and automated inspection among its targets. However,
one point needs to be made clear: we are not faced
here with intentional isolation, which will trigger the
engineering of the self with a view to producing compliance or a process of cellularization to render the subject
docile, as Foucault (1975: 149) understood it. As we saw,
regularization exists only in order to impose a binary
setting regarding the use of the protected space. The
regularizing effects are often unplanned, even undesirable effects of a process of managing spaces, times, flows
and networks. Beyond this, automated control is quite
simply a precondition of contact, a limitation that arises
from mechanicity, not a preparation of the actor for a
subsequent stage.

II.14 The Regularized World

Regrouping several effects of regularization will help set
our analysis in a broader perspective: mutation of the
cultural and the decline of negotiable environments;
desocialization of the legitimate, desocialization of the
individual actor, atomization of the social; destructuring
of various types of stratification and basing social strata
on possession of tokens of access; unintelligibility; and
equality in suspicion.

What image do these colours compose? There will
be no satisfactory answer if we project this image onto
contemporary western society without taking account
of broader social transitions. To seek the importance of

the regularizing effects is to show what they can explain in the society that interests us. In other words, it is a matter of understanding whether regularization is part of a broader context of developments at the level of social organization and identifying the direction in which regularization contributes to that context.

At this stage, it is possible to suppose that a society of regularized individuals would be more a society whose members have identical goals that are formed by seeking ever wider protection of certain desirable objects, services, or situations. Mere knowledge of these fields of desire would thus constitute an axis of social stratification, because there is no other access allowed than that reserved for the legitimated user. For that very reason, one can speak of a compartmentalized world where the excluded actor does not know what is in the sphere, albeit close, to which he is denied access – a social sphere, rather than a society, where everyone is excluded from the majority of the developments that constitute the whole and where it is increasingly difficult to maintain the production of a collective ethos in the isolated actor; a social sphere where the legitimate does not exist as the conclusion of a reasoning, i.e. is no longer *produced by* the social but exclusively *distributed* by remote sources of desocialization; a sphere that, on the contrary, serves only to legitimate its hermetic, unintelligible functioning, placed beyond human cognition. This is, in short, a society of endless – and endlessly renewable – questioning of the condition of the actor and, therefore, a society pervaded by threat.

III. HYPER-REGULARITY: THE CAMERA

"Orthodoxy means not thinking — not needing to think. Orthodoxy is unconsciousness" (Orwell 1949: 46).

The replacement of several dimensions of social control by structures of inspection presents a marked difference in form. The performance of an act of inspection is necessarily explicit because of its institutional content, since it does not question its target in the context of an already existing interaction, but establishes contact to address this target. The exchange is not implicitly governed by norms shared by the questioner and the questioned as members of the same social environment, but by rules specific to the questioner's context that are communicated to the questioned individual. The act of inspection is founded on its own visibility, which must, in one way or another, penetrate into the consciousness of the targeted actor, since compliance cannot be achieved without knowledge of what is required. The inspecting visibility thus sends a twofold message that indicates to its target both the required behaviour and the existence of a device that checks compliance with the rules communicated. If one is not to lose sight of the developments based on this message, it seems necessary to examine not only the precautionary security devices but any inspection structure within the framework of this visibility.

Recent decades have seen developments in industrial societies that have generated an explosive growth of applications in this sector. From all kinds of security guards to "receptionists" at the entrances of buildings and the "face control" imposed on candidates for entry to clubs, there is spectacular growth in the use of methods of inspection.[33] The development of the Internet has created each day new needs for secure contacts and transactions aimed at making the user and her intentions transparent to the institutions of the Web. It is still too early to know how far computerized inspection will go. So, if one now wants to represent the proliferation of inspection by one single element, one has to choose the video surveillance (CCTV) camera. In it one finds condensed the intention of monitoring the behaviour of the targeted actors without their being able to reverse the balance between the observer and the observed, and the means of doing that effectively. The use of surveillance cameras is now so widespread that we associate them almost automatically with any space expected to receive crowds of users (e.g. the subway or the shopping mall), an application that goes far beyond its traditional role as a security device protecting high-security sites (military installations, bank vaults, etc.). Moreover, the falling cost of equipment, accelerated by strong demand (Ocqueteau 1997: 144ff), has made it feasible to install video cameras in medium-sized shops. It is no longer exceptional to encounter CCTV cameras in the local video rental store, the gas-station store,

---

33   The turnover of the "security guard" market in the then twelve EEC
      countries was equivalent to GBP 1,480.62 million in 1988 and growing
      rapidly (Ocqueteau 1992).

or above the cash till in the local café or bakery.[34] What is more interesting is that for some time now video cameras have become an integral part of contemporary architectural design. New residential buildings are routinely equipped with video entry phones, and office buildings are visibly designed to facilitate CCTV surveillance and make access impossible without the visitor being inspected. Meanwhile, a qualitatively different field of application is opening up for the electronic eye. "Quasi-public" spaces, such as car parks, shopping malls or airports are open to the impersonal user and therefore invest in suppressing what can displease or scare him. The rising curve of offences and especially the fear of crime feeds into a dynamics promoting CCTV systems as a reliable and effective solution and makes their installation one of the priorities for the actors in crime prevention, such as the police, local authorities, and businesses.[35] Direct support may even come from the highest level of the state.[36]

The fact that the video camera is indisputably a surveillance device has meant that it was quickly associated with the realm of the panoptic discipline of which Foucault (1975: 195ff.) founded the critique. Thomas Mathiessen (1983) and Stan Cohen have developed that surveillance link, which is no doubt justified. However, there are reasons to think that the build-up of security surveillance in the present conditions produces more varied effects, related to

---

34 Various convergent estimates suggest that there are now more than a million CCTV cameras in France, an average of one for every 60 inhabitants.

35 For a description of this cooperation, see Jones, Newburn and Smith (1994: 252-6).

36 The sympathy of Charles Pasqua, Minister of the Interior in the Balladur government, for surveillance operations took shape in the legislation that he introduced (Act no. 95-73 of January 21, 1995). The British Prime Minister John Major was unequivocal: "We're out to stop the criminal - and the best way to do that is to spot him before he strikes. Closed circuit cameras have proved they can work. So we need more of them wherever crime is high." (quoted by Loveday 1994: 195).

other problematics than those of "hidden discipline." For example, the fact that the video camera is very often one of the high-visibility security devices[37] already predisposes one to look at its role based on threatening perceptions and to associate it with atomizing tendencies. The convergence of several superimposed gazes is hardly surprising in the case of an application as complex as a system of surveillance by transfer and storage of images. It is indeed another novelty of post-industrial society that it is increasingly less reliant on the input of human capacities to achieve its aims. This is not the only point of overlap between the analysis of regularity in the previous chapter and its next stage, hyper-regularity. It is possible to consider that the hyper-regular is merely the product of a closer and more permanent gaze on regularization. By inviting the reader to take account of this latent parallelism, I shall avoid repeating some arguments that I already proposed, which are *mutatis mutandis* valid for surveillance by video camera; so, I can concentrate only on the particular and new aspects of CCTV.

III.1 Surveillance Inverted

In the first place, it is essential to point out that a surveillance device is an interactive mechanism, in the sense that its original logic is expected to be absorbed by the population under surveillance and so attain the dynamics of shaping behaviour. This dimension materializes the role of disciplinary mechanisms as holders of power. Several

---

37 In France, for video recordings on public thoroughfares, the law requires that the public be informed "clearly and permanently of the existence of the video surveillance system and of the authority or person in charge of it" (Act no. 95-73 of January 21, 1995, article 10, §4). In practice, this is extremely rare. Often only the camera is visible, insofar as it is useful as a deterrent.

points of view[38] seem to converge on such an interpretation. However, the similarities should not obscure the differences. A system of surveillance by image transfer is not necessarily intended for a specific population whose behaviour it follows. For example, the inspection devices in the passages of a shopping mall, the subway, or a shop do not monitor a predefined set of persons that owes its existence to the institution itself, as is the case for prisoners or patients; in fact, the actors involved in our case do not share a more or less permanent quality, or even a collective identity. On the contrary, the only element that unites the monitored individuals is their more or less random coexistence within the field of surveillance, an entirely atomized, temporary and freely chosen coexistence. An aspect that sheds light on the role of the device has to do with the fact that we can readily think of conditions in which the camera is used in relation to human absence rather than presence, such as the surveillance systems of warehouses or around airport runways. The first conclusion to which these facts lead us is that the role of the video camera does not relate to surveillance in a positive sense. The system does not seek to confirm at every moment the compliance of the behaviour of the targeted individuals with a detailed, predefined plan of action. It seems to set itself the goal of detecting a breach of the general norms regardless of the institutionalized environment[39] that legitimates or controls the system and its field of application. In this context, the approach taken by the system is negative in that it seeks to detect

---

38   For a critique of the over-insistence on "hidden" and "dispersed" discipline, see Bottoms (1983).

39   The concept of the institution would lose its meaning if it were accepted that a person living alone and having installed a CCTV camera in his dynamics creates an institution; that situation would rather represent the growing institutionalization of the everyday, which is in itself at the centre of late modernity.

the exceptional and not to introduce or verify a partial normality. If this reversal takes us too far from the established view of surveillance, it is also interesting in itself as an independent development. We have here a precautionary security system that acts as a bearer of the social norms in their totality and keeps watch to spot behaviours outside those norms. So the question to be asked about every means of satisfying the growing demands for security is how much it is substituted for social control and with what consequences. Are we, without realizing it, witnessing the beginnings of an "involuntary revolution" that, in an atomized context, tends to connect the norm as such with security measures and extract it from its "natural" space of intersubjectivity?

III.2 Colonized Spaces and Acts

Questions of legitimacy and interaction are inseparably linked to the diffusion of normativity through security. If surveillance by image transfer is organized not around a population or an activity but around a space, this means that it *de facto* transforms the sense of access to that space when it does not altogether change its conditions of accessibility. A space "protected" or "controlled" by video cameras is automatically invested with an aspect that is both threatening and limiting. It is impossible to "use" it as if it were a place exclusively reserved for a single activity (buying provisions, window shopping, waiting for a train, picking up one's car, etc.), because the system acts equally for and against the user at the same time. She is as much a suspect as a potential victim; her actions no longer respond only to the wishes and possibilities that she alone interprets but are *a priori* subject to another parallel, independent interpretation whose principles and source remain unknown. The field of surveillance thus no longer belongs to its user and the institution that legally owns it; a third element slips in between them and colonizes the space that is supposed to exist for the benefit of the institution, no doubt with reference to the user. The camera "privatizes" its field of surveillance[40] in a new way, based on awareness of its existence and on the assimilation of the monitored activity into a system of values that is constantly but invisibly active. So the question of belonging does not arise in relation to the space but, in a remarkable way, in relation to the action as such. This is the context in which we have to place the question of legitimacy. From the moment one crosses the threshold of the monitored field, one's own action no longer refers *de facto* to oneself but develops simultaneously in a context of external justification. Even in the increasingly common conditions where surveillance relates to the most freely accessible places (sidewalks in front of "protected buildings," a city centre, etc.), image transfer generates this new legitimacy because surveillance constitutes a question in itself: if one's presence and actions are being monitored, one must necessarily be in a position to justify them. Therefore, it seems that image transfer establishes a particular kind of self-declared legitimation. However, there is here an apparent difference: the camera does not react, which means the actor also cannot engage in an interaction that confirms or rejects the basis of legitimacy to which she lays claim. The question of the identification of the role of surveillance by image transfer necessarily raises the general problem of the way in which the device acts. Why and how can the system fulfil its functions as a security precaution against victimization of the users and offences in general?

40 Gary Marx (1988: 149) has perspicaciously noted that surveillance leads to the blurring of the distinction between the public and the private.

III.3 The Camera as Mirror

The fact that surveillance in itself contains no element of physical prevention is sufficient to confirm its deterrent character. Even in cases where means for immediate intervention are in place (e.g. direct surveillance by the police or a private security company with agents on the field), the visibility of the cameras serves mainly to *warn the user* of the high probability of detection of a non-authorized act and, presumably, of the unpleasant consequences that this detection entails. If for the gaze behind the camera the role of the device consists in isolating the break with "'normality,'"[41] one should not suppose that this role remains unaltered for the actor under surveillance. On this side, the camera contains in itself a screen with the image of the actor – each actor – in the process of acting; it is both the *receiver* and the *sender* of the image of each individual. This relationship is expressed very clearly at the practical level as in the case of some department stores[42] where the entrance is not marked by the presence of doors, but by screens that show one's own image as one enters, or in the case of banks where the screen showing one's own image is often integrated into the double-door system.

The founding category of the relation of the system to its object is the *reflexivity* that is set up in the actor's viewpoint. This reflexivity is based on the visibility of the camera, combined with the total opacity, for the targeted actor, of the data that the system obtains. In a monitored space, not knowing whether one is seen at a certain

---

41 Video surveillance works on the principle of selection of individuals whom the agent behind the screen evaluates as suspect and decides to track. A whole set of elaborate tactics is used to film the offence (see Ocqueteau and Pottier 1995: 150-7). Automatic image analysis and recording systems operate on the basis of profiles of suspect behaviour that the device is programmed to identify.

42 One example is the Marks and Spencer's store in the Rosny 2 retail center in the outskirts of Paris.

moment is equivalent to being seen at every moment. The ubiquity of the gaze is maintained through its presumption by its object. To act under an alien, unknown, suspicious inspection is not a neutral situation. In sociological terms, it metamorphoses not only the intersubjective group dynamics, but also, through social learning, it leads to the normalization of one's own behaviour within the limits that the actor recognizes as imposed by the social ethos applied to the precise circumstances of his action. The important differentiation, as regards this self-definition of the limits between structures that involve an interaction governed by the socio-cultural norms and those that do not fully obey such norms, such as the bureaucratic systems – or not at all, like technical systems – concerns the actor's ability to test their rigidity through intersubjective mechanisms and adjust his position according to the feedback he receives. The cybernetic model represents *par excellence* this level of social interaction where, as in a game of tennis, the decision is both precise and original, and perfectly adapted both to the actions of the other players and to one's own aspirations. However, in the socio-cognitive universe, neither the rules of the game nor the boundaries are predefined; they are set by the play itself.

III.4 Abnormality and Asociality

While the machine generally substitutes its rigidity for relationships that are constantly forming and makes the contact non-negotiable, these precautionary security measures, in which the human being is not the final link,[43] introduce a mediation of social experience such that a

---

43   I refer here to the variety of security messages that are not communicated person-to-person, i.e. any mediated and desocializing contact that does not have the margin of full social interaction. The form of these messages can range from stickers on car windows warning of an alarm to safety advertisements and surveillance cameras.

logic of risk is internalized by the actor. At another level, precaution regarding victimization can trigger this internalization, which is conveyed not only via threat, but also via suspicion, i.e. the particular threat of being considered a source of threat, which is above all the case for the likely perpetrator of an offence. Ackermann, Dulong, and Jeudy (1983: 102) predicted that electronic surveillance systems "through their multiplication will reduce the social role of the city or even lead to a total death of 'urban life'. For it is indeed the city that becomes a space of threat, uncertainty, chance, unpredictability...."

The effect of the video surveillance camera operates deep inside the process of internalization. Apart from the more general effects that precautionary security measures produce, the reflexivity of the domain of surveillance is marked by some crucial specificities. First, the act no longer belongs totally to the actor but takes place in parallel "elsewhere" under the eyes of an observer looking for something exceptional, in particular, some abnormality that will trigger attention and concentrate the gaze. It is not important at this level to know whether it is a human observer or an image analysis software that is automatically activated according to preconceived criteria, whether it be the speed of a vehicle on the highway or that of users in relation to one another in subway corridors.[44] Thus, the observed individual finds himself on the stage of the security theatre, where, as on any stage, it is mainly the degree of unexpectedness that defines the spectator's focus. However, the actor's aspiration here is not to become the protagonist, but to remain

---

44 In the Paris subway, eight out of ten cases where staff are called to intervene are detected by the self-activation of the image analysis system, which automatically brings up on the screen situations that it "recognizes" as abnormal (someone running, approaching the edge of the platform, etc.). Less sophisticated domestic systems can be triggered automatically by simple presence in a protected space and bring the image up on the TV screen.

the "extra," effaced by the banality of his anonymous transit of the screen. "Being normal" is a conviction the value of which becomes relative on a stage peopled by atomized actors whose only common point is that they are all under observation. *Appearing normal* is what really counts.

The intensity of this demand can of course vary according to the modalities of the relationship between the observed and the system. Habit can lead one to "forget" the gaze of the camera, and the danger of being observed without knowing it has led to the legal imposition of notices, pointing out the use of surveillance systems. However, the propagation of their use indicates rather that the installation of surveillance in everyday experience merges forgetting with vigilance into the presumption that one is observed. It would be somewhat naïve to suppose that the electronic gaze is neutral for the monitored actor, just as it would be to think that the socio-cognitive mechanisms are not able to integrate the condition of surveillance into the normality of lived experience. What is interesting is to see how such an integration is possible in the specific context of surveillance. A society's "learning by doing" in relation to electronic surveillance comes through the relationship between the private self and the public self, and more precisely between the *praxic act*, i.e. the act *hic et nunc* that belongs to the present of the actor, and the *observed act*, the one that takes place as an image on a screen and which, wrenched from the control of the actor, belongs to the observer, to be subject to his judgment and satisfy his criteria of normality. The gulf between these two facets is not as simple as their parallel unfolding suggests. If the praxic act constitutes a social event in the sense that it both understands and reacts to its context (pushing the trolley in the supermarket, waiting in line at the bank, etc.), the observed act is the utilitarian component of an institutionalized process, the aim of which is precisely to isolate the act from its social context[45] and examine it from another point of view. The difference specifically concerns this transformation of belonging and thereby, of the distance between society at large and the security control station. The act derives its meaning from its insertion in this context, but its "sociality" is not exhausted by that: it is deepened by its *non-existence* elsewhere, in space or time, i.e. by the impossibility of detaching the act from its present. The sociality of the praxic act is grounded in the fact that it can never be repeated as such, it dies with its context, and any subsequent reference to it is only an interpretation, doubtful by definition. There remains the narrative of myth, testimony, or history, already subject to its own present, which tends to '"reconstruct'" the act. As the receivers of such narratives are well aware, they are definitively set in their own time and therefore the act is lost for ever as praxic reality; it exists only as a reflection of the new present of the narrative toward the past. *The social is unitemporal* but the technical is not. Repetition is its fundamental capacity. The technology of the image gives the possibility not only of watching, but also of "recreating" the watching.

III.5 Transtemporality

Whereas in photographic recording the image and its storage are one and the same, the electronic image can be as present as the praxic reality that it reproduces. But, it offers two advantages: it can be immediately transmitted over any distance, and it can be much more easily stored. Post-industrial populations are accustomed to the possibility

---

45   Cameras now available on the market make it possible to detect a person's eye colour at a distance of 400 yards; see for example *The Independent*, July 6, 1994.

of creating their own archives of these images.[46] Given the level of diffusion of the electronic media, it would be rare to find individuals in the post-industrial world who have attained the age of reason without being aware of the widespread recording and storage of electronic images. Replays of spectacular or ambiguous moments in sport, video reports recorded before transmission of the news, and snapshots from different stages in the story or a life are just three of the countless ways in which stored images appear on the screen, conspicuously breaking into the present of the spectacle.

This is the framework in which surveillance by image transfer develops its potential, the terms "archive" or "CCTV footage" often being displayed to underline the technical storage capacity of the system. This capacity expresses in a new way the invariable element of any precautionary device, namely its "superfluous effect," which consists in processing individuals and circumstances that have no close connection with the likelihood of committing the act that the precautionary measures target in each case. On the grounds of reducing the probability of an offence, the video camera subjects every actor to its surveillance, refusing him an individual evaluation, and so contributes to the collapse of several interactive processes that converge on what I have called the "demise of decent people." In fact, the precautionary superfluous effect constitutes the key element of the distinction between the utilitarian goals of the device and its true social consequences.

Video surveillance is becoming ever more widespread and common. That is why one needs to stress some of its

---

46 According to Eurostat, 90 percent of households in the European Union (EU) have a television set, and the rate of video recorder ownership is over 50 percent in some countries. The recent popularization of the multimedia environment opens quasi-unlimited scope for the reception and storage of digital or digitized images.

aspects in order to detect the reflexivity of the relationship
between the system, the observed act, and the monitored
actor. In some sectors, it is becoming less rare to see one's
own image on a screen. The clients of several French
banks, for example, often experience this. In general, the
entrance to a branch has a double door "mantrap" that
makes going in a two-stage process – two electronically
controlled, reinforced doors can only open alternately
(one cannot open without the other being closed); all the
client can do is signal his intention to enter by pressing
a button; he cannot influence the operation or the coordination of the system. Each client must enter alone,
with his face visible, in accordance with the instructions
displayed (helmets cannot be worn). He remains in the
"steel cage" between the doors for a few seconds. A screen
shows him that he is being watched by a video camera.
This two-stage entry process is very obviously designed
to bar the way to potential offenders. However, it would
be absurd to suppose that a bank robber would present
himself with mask and shotgun in front of the device,
waiting for the door to be opened for him. It would,
therefore, be more accurate to suppose that the device
is there to slow the exit rather than block the entry. Even
in its mechanical dimension, independent of surveillance
technology, we have here a structure entirely devoted to
showing that security measures are in place and thus to
deter the potential offender. Every client is treated in the
same way. In short, this is a regulating procedure with
very high rigidity and visibility.

If access management fulfils a practical role, and
thereby achieves its deterrent function, the projection of one's own image in real time can only have the
purpose of warning. It represents, in the first place, the
application of a gaze monitoring the actor's behaviour,

i.e. a reinforcement of the awareness of surveillance. However, habituation to the media can reveal another dimension. This preliminary inspection would be of little use if it could not be related to *the time of the offence*. The isolation of each client to whom his own image is addressed takes on a crucial meaning if this client is the one whose presence justifies the installation of the device – the perpetrator of an offence. It, therefore, goes without saying that if the recording and storing of the image are so easy, the message relates to the *identification* of each individual and not (or very little) to the preliminary evaluation of his intentions. This logic is not specific to the recording of images but extends to surveillance applications in general. For example, the introduction of the electronic tag to make confinement at home an alternative to prison follows the same principle. It is a reflexive imprisonment, self-imposed on the basis that the system *will know* if a breach of compliance has taken place and that punishment will ensue (Fay 1993).

So what is displayed is that the surveillance device and any institution linked to it know that a specific person is there at a specific moment, and *detailed knowledge of this moment remains stored indefinitely*. If the institution concerned discovers a particular problem, even *ex post facto*, the image can be retrieved by reference to its time, and be watched a thousand times, meticulously analyzed and slowed down to reveal all the details that an otherwise banal and neutral appearance contains. This process marks the dramatic gulf between the praxic act and the observed act that the electronic surveillance sets up. Through its stored image, the observed act becomes indisputably not only transspatial, but also *transtemporal*. Instead of being normally wiped from the memory of its author, it will continue to exist in the memory of the system for as long as the institution sees fit.[47]

The transtemporality of surveillance is a development that inaugurates a new way of looking at the everyday, since for the monitored individual it raises the question, among others, of the ownership of the act and of her identity. Outside this general problematic, the theme of reflexivity takes an even more complicated form. These developments bear witness to the advent of a new preventive security tactic, corresponding to another perspective by the actor on her own actions. We have here a view of the present through the projection onto the future that is brought about by an inspection that is preliminary to the act but that refers to a time yet to come, which deprives the present of any meaning other than that of a retrospective examination situated in the future. The content of the behaviour is indefinitely suspended by the surveillance device. Moreover, it is the continuation of this suspension that confirms the normality of the act. Thus, all positive certainty remains by definition inaccessible. Only the breaking of the suspension by moving to the stage of inquiry can provide the one possible certainty: that of suspicion. One sees here the unbridgeable gap the actor has every interest in filling to avoid the questioning of her status. Even more pressing is the awareness that the behaviour acquires a transtemporal dimension and thus freezes the act in time, excluding the possibility of later correction by the social practices of compensation: taking an object from a shop and managing to put it back later would equate to the possibility of allowing someone to maintain it was always there, an argument that a replay of the videotape of the day in question refutes without further discussion. The

---

47   Theoretically, recordings made on public thoroughfares must be erased within a month "except in the case of inquiry into an observed offence" (Act 95-73 of January 21, 1995, Article 10, §4) but no administrative checks on compliance with the law are provided for.

recorded image constitutes an unequivocal proof *in itself* and makes each of its viewers a witness. The diffusion of the manifestations of this absolute force is rapidly gaining ground in contemporary societies, and not only in the context of "trial by media." Judges and juries increasingly watch videos of the acts they have to judge, and confirmation by image is leading to more guilty verdicts and much more severe sentences.[48] Increasingly, major cases involving phobogenic offences will be solved by the diffusion through the media of recordings of the suspects. Very often, the images come from systems that are there for reasons that have nothing to do with the acts in question (CCTV cameras in a supermarket, a shopping mall, or a subway station)[49]. If we suppose that we are only at the start of an information feed-back effect between the actor and his image, it is already clear that the observed act is not only transspatial and transtemporal, but also asocial. It constitutes definitive, indelible, autonomous, and precise proof that the act took place in a given place at a given time, a proof that renders the use of socio-cognitive means of constructing the past superfluous, if not suspect.

---

48 The emotional effect on the jury of seeing footage of a violent crime is clearly very important; and "there is little point [in] arguing against video evidence" (*The Independent*, July 6, 1994).

49 The majority of the recent most publicized crimes have been resolved with the aid of video recordings broadcast on TV. Sequences from private video surveillance systems operating near the premises concerned (entrances, sidewalks, etc.) were shown on TV in the cases of the Warrington bombings in March 1993 and the car bomb outside the Harrods store in London, for which "the perpetrators were arrested four hours after the film was broadcast" (*The Times*, April 14, 1994); also for the 1993 Graff Diamonds robbery (*The Times*, July 16, 1993) and the case of Colin Ireland, who killed five gay men before being identified from a recording by the security system of the London Underground, where he was seen with his last victim (*The Times*, July 2, 1993). A shopping mall video recording was also crucial in the case of James Bulger, a toddler killed by two other children; the event convinced Liverpool City Council of the usefulness of CCTV surveillance and two years later a system was installed to cover the city centre and a four-mile-wide area around it (*The Times*, July 6, 1994).

The narrative of the electronic image is there, unalterable, open to no revision; it discredits not just some interpretations but interpretation as such. While any human testimony can be subject to evaluative questions ("Is she telling the truth?", "Did he see everything?") the videotape removes their *raison d'être*. Thus, while it is always possible to alter the praxic act by mechanisms that play on identity and culture, *the recorded act is irreversible.* From this point of view, entry into the field of surveillance of a video camera means crossing the threshold of a new, desocialized world in which the act remains always present, since it is always possible to integrate it into the present by its representation, even if it belongs to the past. This development is no doubt part of the breaking of the temporal axis and the blurring of its stages in post-industrial societies. But, as regards the narrower field of normativity, it marks the entry into a new era of inspection performed by capture of behaviour and the possibility of analyzing it in the future. Even when it is not accompanied by a screen addressing the targeted actor in real time, the video camera clearly displays its message: do nothing suspicious; we know who you are, and we shall have conclusive evidence that you are the one who did it. As the present cannot assume a representation of the complete, immediate, autonomous lived experience, it evaporates in hypotheses that seek to justify and legitimate its content against the weight of inspection. The key to this colonization of the present by the future as regards surveillance by the electronic image is, as we have seen, the '"normality"' of the behaviour.

III.6 Autoscopy

We should, however, take account of the social dynamics that will use all its means to win back its territory and immunize its own present against all uncertainty. These two antagonistic perspectives meet in the field of surveillance where they reach a compromise that balances their forces. Thus, the normality of behaviour becomes the crucial factor in establishing stability and reducing the threatening potential of future events. Appearing normal becomes the vital instrument for stabilizing one's own present, controlling it, and reintegrating it into the actor's field of decision. At the level of the wider society, this motivation clearly concerns the very possibility of forming social representations, since the suspension of the present by negative future probabilities shatters the definitive and certain character of the everyday interaction that is in turn indispensable for shaping the formation of a collective ethos. The wish to appear normal thus emerges as a factor of the social. In this context, normality becomes the main means of defence for both the individual and society against the development of devices and structures of inspection. How can this defence make itself concrete? Direct individual or collective opposition could be a first reaction.

Indeed, the issue is often approached from the point of view of individual freedom and the protection of privacy,[50] and enters the public arena in this form. This apparent problematic is based on an invisible edifice. If this were not the case, the neoconservative position would be indisputably valid in asserting that only those who have suspect intentions have reason to oppose the growth of surveillance or inspection measures. Yet, without being analyzed, the experience of inspection in itself arouses

---

50   However, it is noteworthy that when the question is posed in terms of perceived utility, the results can be surprising and sometimes worrying. Jowell et al. (1991: 194) found not only that 40 percent of the British population agree with the installation of cameras in soccer stadia, but that 40 percent also approve of the filming of political demonstrations.

opposition in society.[51] This opposition often appears opaque and "irrational" to institutions; the theses put forward here can also be read as explanations. To understand the visible collective reaction, one should combine it with the possible strategy, which remains in the shadow of public or private consciousness,[52] but which is nonetheless the only means of defence. One is indeed expected to give the inspection structure what it asks for. If the central point is to integrate oneself as much as possible into the monitored mass, the problem presents itself as an exercise in preparing for the practice of this normality and the suppression of behaviour that could be perceived as exceptional. One could thus speak of an *autoscopy*, a self-control preceding external inspection that is set up as contact with the inspecting structures progresses.[53] If this proposition seems to be a hypothesis that is difficult to verify, it is, in fact, only an application of the structuring of social control in a new and different context. It is self-evident that the mechanisms of social control are integrated into social values and identities. Thus, they establish models of "normal" and not "'imposed'" action. The external constraints on behaviour that do not derive from coercive violence indeed operate through the aware-

---

51 This opposition remains, however, individual, perhaps because of the intense fear of victimization experienced in an isolated way, and because of the banalization of surveillance. The attempts to start up a social movement on this issue, such as the creation in Paris of the collective "Smile, you're on camera," have clearly failed.

52 In terms of social psychology, the behaviour of groups is interpreted either through self-awareness as a group member or as a result of a reduction in self-control. The private awareness and the public awareness that correspond to these two models are differentiated in terms of consequences (Abrams and Brown 1989). Surveillance seems to lead to a fusion of these two types of awareness in a compliance anchored outside the self.

53 It is perhaps more useful to speak here of autoscopy and not conditioning, since it is a matter of self-adaptation through future projections which constitute *unintentional* effects of the device.

ness that the actor develops of them and the preparation of her behaviour so as to satisfy this awareness. But, while social norms derive from the point of view of others and a practice that takes account of it, inspection relates to the point of view of a suspicious third party and the electronic surveillance of a practice that assimilates in advance the demands of the gaze of the camera.

The problem that emerges through this internalization is to conceive it in its new and particular framework of a desocialized, even asocial structure. The way in which the mechanical rigidity of inspection in general – and electronic surveillance, in particular – influences behaviour cannot follow the usual model of internalization of the social norms processed by intersubjectivity. A first observation concerns the splitting of the register of the normality of behaviour into two currents, in accordance with the development of two points of view around it. While the normative order as such could not exist outside of the framework of intersubjective interaction until the advent of electronic technology, its mutated form is emerging at a growing rate. In order to be defined, thus come into existence, the norm imposed within an institution or applied in society would presuppose interaction between participants. It is not a question of denying the possibility of planning social norms and of applying the planned norms, a stance that would largely deny the existence of the political as such. The point is to make it clear that it is intersubjectivity that gives rise to, modifies, and suppresses the norm as an equilibrium among the participants: the "other," like the self, is both bearer and subject of the normative and nothing can establish an influence of this sort outside of the interactive relationship. The advent of inspection breaks this social closure by setting up a point of view external to the interaction, which is situated in a third-party context. With an approach that is minimalist in terms of application but effective in terms of control, the camera realizes in an unexpected way the proposition of the reduction of authority to its necessary core, as Rogers and Skinner conceived it: "According to present knowledge, the only authority necessary is the authority to establish certain qualities of the interpersonal relationship" (Rogers and Skinner 1956: 1065). However, it would be more than debatable to assert that the gaze of the camera leads to the utopia of a non-normative environment because it is freeing its targets from the strictly social norm.

The subject of this gaze is neither participant nor neutral. Above all, it is unknown and unidentifiable. Who is the true bearer of the gaze of a camera? Probably, all those who might have the power and interest to access the recorded image (the security staff, the store manager, the researcher, the employer, the witness, the prosecutor, the member of the jury, the journalist, the future historian, etc.). The observer is manifold, distant, and dispersed in the institutional archipelago and so cannot be identified by the targeted individual. The gaze of surveillance is not only transspatial and transtemporal, but also transpersonal and transintentional. It can cease at the moment of its creation or extend indefinitely without ever being activated until its destruction, but it can also be shown on the evening's TV news. Moreover, it may be the fleeting object of the bored glance of a security employee or never be seen, but it may also be meticulously analyzed. In any case, it is impossible to associate this third-party gaze with a person, an institution, or a set of norms, i.e. to situate its demands in a social context. However, what is demanded persists: an overall self-imposed normality, paradoxical in that it no longer refers to others directly, but nonetheless rigid and effective through its projection into the future.

This third-party, asocial"hypernorm" constitutes the contribution of mechanical machine-mediated inspection and thus founds a new paradigm of normality that is not based on intersubjective interpellation but on the uncertainty of intrasubjective hypotheses.[54] Its content is unambiguous: appear normal, don't stand out. Paradoxically, it seems that what is weakened in one way is strengthened in the other, since the integration of each targeted individual into the monitored set to which he or she belongs (and this increasingly means society in general) would automatically mean a reference to the already existing social norms. But, things are not so simple, on the one hand because in this way it is the monitoring gaze that legitimates the norm and not the reverse; and on the other hand, because if we have this new motivation to comply with the norms, we must do so with the asocial rigidity that it imposes on us and only to the point of covering external aspects of this compliance. To situate these developments in a context of atomization, one could simply say that we are witnessing the birth of a tendency in which the norm has no other dimension than that of the means of the diffusion of an inspecting gaze; this is because the actor is no longer questioned *by* other actors but only *in relation* to the other actors by the inspecting process. In other words, we have here not only a mechanism of reinforcing norms, but also of suppression of the values attached to them, and thereby a practice of homogeneity that establishes normality as a unique and absolute value, justified only by its utilitarian role, a normality for the first time stripped of any social support or justification.

---

54   We thus have a profound break in the intersubjective foundation of the nature and legitimacy of the norm, as described by Habermas (1991: 889): "That a norm is established in practice means inversely that the validity claim with which it appears is recognized by those affected, and this intersubjective recognition grounds the social validity of the norm." A third-party element now enters this process in a way not seen before.

III.7 Hyper-regularity

In the asocial context where autoscopic preparation is supposed to operate, the tendencies that have been described so far necessarily move towards a coherent, concrete model of action simply because the creation of such a model is imperative for the actor. In the first place, the cultural content of intersubjective contact becomes superfluous since, in the field of surveillance, it is not supported by any motivation. The importance of social practices of negotiation thus declines and the monitored actor no longer tends to focus on them. They are no longer decisive either for his actions or for his identity and biographical project. However, this means that the process of continuous renewal of the social norms underperforms. Moreover, in the absence of its *raison d'être*, the normativity becomes rigid, retaining only its external shell but not a living, mobile body. The consequence of this "formal" normative practice is that the actor can no longer negotiate the limits of his behaviour and orient himself in the way that corresponds to his values. Formal normality thus signals the advent of centripetal tendencies, hostile to the practice of liminal behaviours that form new spaces for the normal. So, it seems we are moving toward an adequate explanation of the existence of a hard core of homogeneous behaviour in post-industrial societies that runs through large parts of the social classes and the categories of population that are defined according to more partial factors (age, gender, ethnic origin, lifestyle, education, etc.). Under the weight of autoscopy, formal normality is in itself equivalent to access to a social status, since being capable of adhering to it proves the entitlement and skill to be socially integrated. This status is clearly not the end of the process of social stratification, but it is increasingly its foundation. Because it is so important to appear normal, it seems justified for the actor to tend toward the core that categorically identifies a behaviour with the desired normality. Given the formality of intersubjective contact, the means and motive to explore the external margins of behaviour in society are reduced. In this framework, the act no longer carries the tendency to negotiate and possibly increase the influence of the values carried by its author. It begins to embody the *adherence* of its subject to the predominant praxic models more than the internalization of the social values of which these models are one of the many expressions. These circumstances raise an important question with regard to the emergence of the new mechanisms of building social identities. For we see here the probability that these mechanisms will move away from the attribution of value-based justifications to the acts committed, and replace them with a reflex that detects the assimilation of one's acts to those of the other actors. If the only "value" that is necessary to link the actor to others bears on the recognition of the praxic context and integration with it, why should the actor continue to provide value-based justifications for his own exclusive use? Individual identity will not use means to constitute itself that cannot be cashed at the social stock exchange – which means that the more the practices of inspection are propagated, the more identity and behaviour will fall back on a deculturated core of formal normality.

In these conditions, one can wonder about the fate of the external margins of behaviour not practised on the periphery of this core. In a praxic context, one can express this condition of the threshold, this "liminality," via the difference between the authorized and the habitual. While the law seeks to lay down a line between the absolutely permitted and the absolutely forbidden, interaction in society is understood by all as relative. This relativity is expressed in the range of judgements on what is normal. Depending on each observer's point of view, legal behaviours, like dying one's hair green or walking around eating an ice cream when it is snowing, may appear more or less normal. This testifies to the existence of social control and the possibilities of following several strategies within it, depending on the desired objective. However, it would be a mistake to associate the role of video cameras to that of a social environment or even a peer group, given that *the camera takes no position; it does not recommend any behaviour but the assimilation of each actor's behaviour to that of the others,* i.e. to the model of normality that she recognizes around her. Thus, electronic surveillance becomes the mirror of an ethos that is particular in each case: that of the supermarket customer, car park user, bank customer, etc. It is by projecting this ethos onto each actor, by reflecting the normality established by the other targets, that it leads to the self-regulation of the behaviour of all. In conditions of electronic surveillance, personal strategies lose their meaning, and autoscopic control becomes the only means of forming any cognitive principle for the management of one's own acts. The asocial rigidity of the device informs the autoscopic control as to the centripetal formality of the behaviour that this control must prepare. In other words, the centripetal tendency concerns a know-how that *precedes* the act, because *the marginal act in the field of surveillance has none of its social utilities* but only responds negatively to security considerations. Thus, the only difference in its meaning and the only meaning in its difference refers to dangerousness, which the device detects as abnormality and reflects as fear among the other actors. It seems that the reflexivity of the relation between the subject and the object of the observation leads to the desocialization of the observed act itself. On the other hand, under the pressure of the autoscopic dynamics, the limit of the field in which this asocial act is set always tends to move toward the centre. The criteria of homogeneity and dangerousness are the only parameters of the meaning of the behaviour within the field of surveillance; this combination renders both inactive and meaningless the margin of the socially liminal behaviour that could otherwise have continued to place itself on the threshold of the acceptable. This configuration would represent a static condition if one could envisage a given and stable core and periphery that would both continue as such after the suppression of a field of liminal behaviours. But, the reproduction of this schema is a dynamic condition. What can be distinguished as liminal will constitute a new periphery, and so on, moving toward the establishment of a homogeneity that is ever more precise and refined in its details. Each new margin of the mode of action atrophies because it is not nourished by a social practice capable of keeping it active. From this point of view, the continuous pressure of the inspecting rigidity provokes each time the atrophy of a new outer ring of action and brings the boundaries of permitted behaviour closer to an increasingly dense centre of normality. In the framework of inspection, desocialization is performed by this hypernormality in which each actor is expected to ensure his alignment on the demands of the inspection system by bringing his behaviour ever closer to that of others, to avoid triggering the "interest" of the device and to maximize certainty about his own non-dangerous status.

It would clearly be very difficult to verify these hypernormalizing tendencies if one had no proof of their presence in the structuring of the inspecting device. The fact that the use of video surveillance cameras often coexists with the regulating process helps to clarify the reception of electronic surveillance. The question relating to the issue of regulating structures concerns the effect of surveillance on a collective behaviour entirely embedded in the design of the device itself. At the airport, in a department store or in a supermarket, one follows precise, homogeneous flows, often without any alternative. These are pre-conditions for the functioning of a regularizing structure. Who dares to think what would happen in the subway network if a saboteur were to alter the signage so that opposite flows of passengers came face to face?[55] This sensitivity to precision is not without its normative effects. Taking account of the superfluous effect of the device, the combination of surveillance and regularization for the overwhelming majority of users serves only to reinforce adherence to the process of regularization, of verifying that one is subject to its action, and that one will be sanctioned if one tries to avoid it. From this state of affairs, two answers can be derived: first, the effectiveness of surveillance depends on the structuring of the environment that constitutes its field; second, this necessary link exists because it comes from the possibility of isolating the actor or act that does not resemble the rest. That is why the hypernormal context can be seen as a general tendency of the set of covering all different means of inspection. Hypernormality arises, however, as an imposition of asocial regularities and not of social norms and undermines the norms in favour of the regularities. Strictly speaking, this is a process that, on the one hand, increasingly narrows the spectrum of the actor's behaviour and, on the other hand, "wraps" the act in preconceived, pre-recognizable, asocial schemas, i.e. regularizes it. For these reasons, it would be more exact to refer to this effect of inspection as "hyper-regularity."

55   From this point of view the network forms a gigantic exercise in reading and interpreting signage for the user, who is thus disoriented by definition. The signage follows the logic of flow management, often in clear contradiction of the principle of the shortest route. In the major subway stations, for example, the passenger "by-passes" points where flows intersect, zigzagging rather than heading directly toward his destination.

Graph 1: Hyper-regularity

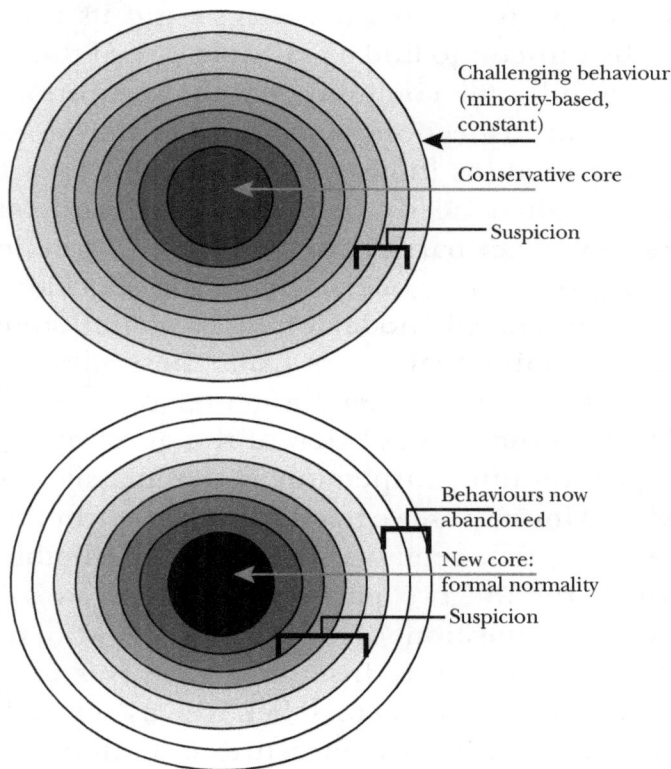

Challenging behaviour
(minority-based,
constant)

Conservative core

Suspicion

Behaviours now
abandoned

New core:
formal normality

Suspicion

Hyper-regularity: Narrowing down
the limits of normality

III.8 Power, Distance, Probability

It seems very likely that hyper-regularity is indeed
a phenomenon that extends beyond the domain of
inspection and more generally beyond the relationship
between probability and certainty. However, within the
limits of this discussion, by looking at the other side of
the device one can already observe the seeds of a more
general quality that arises from hyper-regularizing
structures. It is a matter of situating the inspection and
its consequences in terms of power. Even for those who

are strongly inclined to attribute all power to a centre conscious of its dominant strength and its interests, it would be difficult to find a plausible line of thought that links around some common goal the institutions which make use of inspection measures. On the other hand, the concern of institutions to use these means to meet their individual needs (e.g. the speed and precision offered by ticket barriers or anti-theft magnetic gates) and the growing fear of crime combine in a clear, repetitive but atomized model of their commitment. The important point that arises from these circumstances is that inspection is indeed a matter of *individual positioning* from the point of view of the questioner.

If proliferating inspection is the massive effect of individual initiatives, we need to consider whether there is one thing that remains stable and intelligible simultaneously for the two participants in the relationship (questioner/questioned) regardless of who occupies these roles each time. Installing measures to confirm that a certain set of actors behaves as wanted would not be a novelty if these measures operated within the social; this condition would require the questioner to be manifestly present, in one way or another, as a social and communicative entity. This is exactly the factor that the present structures of automatic inspection reverse. While the questioned actor becomes totally and permanently transparent in space and time, the questioner remains invisible and unknown, as do the operations of the device. Thus, the operator manages the act from a distance without being subject to any risk, shielded from any danger and even from any influence that the actor could exert on him. The camera will record the line of clients or the hold-up with identical precision and transfer the whole local experience except for the fear. Like a latex glove, it allows probing without the risk of contagion. This disequilibrium is the basis of the questioner's advantage over the questioned, who is subject not only to the praxic dangers themselves, but also to the risk of suspicious judgment. If the position of the one is certain and unambiguous, the position of the other takes on meaning precisely through the uncertainty that surrounds it, of which the sole master is the questioner. Their relationship is based on a "one-way interaction" that serves exclusively to render one party ever more transparent and the other ever more opaque. The basis of this unidirectionality is formed by the praxic and above all eclectic *distance* of the relationship. Being close to the act but remote from its consequences forms a new vehicle of power, because although distance constitutes a historical parameter of the realization of power, it comes up against the limit set by the everyday, the control of which has always required visible and sustained proximity. The intervention of the machine, transferring only the part of reality that facilitates inspection, radically changes the configuration of the field and sets in motion another dynamics as regards the axis of power. It is now the balance of accessibility and vulnerability that will define what is at stake in terms of domination and will decide what constitutes power. While this does not in itself justify a revision of the structuring of all domination, it is clear at this stage, for the first time in the domain of control, that power concerns not the detection of the sanctioned act or the right to define the criteria for characterizing an act as such but, well before these stages, touches on the *probability* of this act being committed in the future. The introduction of independence between the certainty of the event and its future realization requires the enlargement of the categories of analysis of the social in order to bring this new space to light. However, one development is already visible: the birth of the management of probability as a reality that is possible, and therefore as valid as the present reality, sets the problematic of power in a qualitatively different context. Focusing on probability frees the process from the constraint of reference to facts and enables it to make what has not yet existed (and may never exist) a '"power -relevant incident..." The mediation of the present by the future thus corresponds to an anticipatory and preliminary treatment of the possible by a disequilibrium of power, which, for the first time, can autonomize itself from the social as such by colonizing the projections that concern the social.

IV THE OTHER DANGERIZED: ISOLATION AND THE FEAR OF VICTIMIZATION

"The inner city," "the housing estate" – in France "*la zone*," "*la banlieue*" – contains the great fears of the "socially included" members of post-industrial society. The insistence on the theme is often irresistible: unemployment, drugs, violence, foreigners, crime, and poverty. The media narrative is simple enough to interest its reader by placing him before the hard core of the social threat. Here is the quintessence of "falling," the large-scale consequence of failure or the dead-end for a working life or blocked career. We may think we are shielded from the danger of our own precariousness, but it is impossible to escape from the awareness of the precariousness of others. If our own precariousness threatens us individually through the destabilization of our socio-occupational environment,[56] that of other people

---

56   For a description of how the middle classes perceive the legitimacy of their own way of life, see Ehrenreich (1989).

points us toward the control and isolation of the population "'contaminated'" by the various social diseases. The first element of this control lies in the very perception of the question.

American cities have their "no-go" areas where only the "streetwise" can survive, as the media never cease to remind us; but the awareness of the "social threat" is also implanted in Europe.[57] No doubt concern for security against violence and theft is mounting. In 1994, 95 percent of the British population was afraid of crime against their persons or their living spaces, and 93 percent said their worry about "crime" had increased in recent years. These percentages had remained at about the same level for a long time.[58] However, the usual approach, which treats what is called "fear of crime"[59] or "sense of insecurity"[60] as a distinct domain of experience, does little to advance the understanding of the phenomenon or its role in the wider social context.

In the first place, we lack a term to describe the phenomenon with analytical rigour: "Crime" is not a concept that corresponds to ontological reality. "Crime is not the object but the product of a criminal policy"

---

57 While it is true that in Europe people do not like to think that the situation is comparable to the United States, a legitimate question calls for an answer: "Today, no senior police officer, no local authority and no Government minister would or could admit that no-go districts existed.... How else do you describe an area which taxi drivers refuse to serve, where doctors are advised to seek police protection before making house calls, and which the police themselves will only visit in numbers?" (*The Independent on Sunday*, April 17, 1994).

58 In 1987 90 percent and in 1989 87 percent also said that their worry had increased (MORI 1994).

59 For different stances on the definition of the "fear of crime," see Williams and Dickinson 1993: 34-5.

60 Translator's note: The prevalent term for the fear of crime is "sentiment d'insécurité" in France. This work introduced "peur de victimation" as a technical term, which is now widely used by the French social science community.

(Hulsman 1985: 33). It is a legal category, a product of law. The association of the notion of crime with a certain type of activities, very often limited to illegal physical violence, and not with other forms of behaviour such as white collar criminality, both demonstrates and strengthens the high visibility of illegal activity linked to the disadvantaged[61] and the masking of the gravity of the crime committed by other classes. As Box (1983: 45) puts it, we see here a political will to "increase the likelihood of criminalizing poor, oppressed and sometimes maladjusted individuals while leaving the rich corporate executive free to operate inside and outside the law." Braithwaite and Fisse (1987: 234) observe that corporate crime is much less visible than its consequences would justify, and that this invisibility is politically constructed: "[...] corporate crime causes more material harm and damage than street crime. However, we know that it is politically and fiscally unrealistic to hope that our generation will see an allocation of public resources to cut corporate crime even remotely comparable to that devoted to street crime" (Braithwaite and Fisse 1987).

So it seems difficult to suppose that an individual who is "afraid of crime" fears that a company is producing false invoices. As British MP Sir Ivan Lawrence put it, "people are afraid of being assaulted, not of fraud in the City." On the other hand, the "sense of insecurity" refers to a much wider socio-cognitive spectrum; it constitutes a convergence of uncertainties generated in various sectors, and the fear of being the victim of illegal behaviour is only one aspect of this. The fear of being a victim must therefore be understood in connection with the person's *private life*, since it is, firstly, the body and the spaces that are exclu-

---

61   In spite of persistent data showing that the overwhelming majority of known violent crime is experienced by the poor, fear continues to grow among the other classes (Smith 1983: 124; Box 1983: 2).

sively intended for it that are the target of the projected
threat.[62] Only that which is part of our self-identification
process acquires the value needed to create a permanent
pole of anxiety. This link can be clearly seen in the case
of burglary without physical injury. The parallelism of the
trauma with that of rape constantly surfaces (Ackermann,
Dulong and Jeudy 1983: 41). The awareness that a stranger,
who will often remain unknown, has laid hands on one's
personal objects is felt as an indirect bodily contact, a prof-
anation by another person of what is sacred to oneself,
and therefore a violation of the integrity of one's personality. When victimization is seen as a projection into the
whole perceptual universe of the victim, it becomes clear that
fear covers at the same time all aspects of violence or other
forms of aggressive behaviour that threaten a person in a
private or intimate way. Research has only recently begun
to integrate this aspect of things by talking about "percep-
tually associated" offences. This is the case, for example,
with the "shadow of rape" in relation to the fear of crime
in women, "who are more afraid of non-sexual crime but
this is largely due to their fear of sexual crimes" (Ferraro
1995: 100; see also Hough and Mayhew 1985: 41; Smith
1989). It, therefore, seems more legitimate to consider
that the blanket fear of the behaviour of others is based on
the subject who feels it and not on legal definitions. For
lack of a better term, I shall use "fear of victimization"[63]
to refer to the experience of a threat related to an illegal
behaviour concerning the integrity of the intimate sphere
of the person.

---

62 Fear is each time the feeling of a socially specific subject. This is why
    simplistic interpretations that make an absolute link between the emer-
    gence of fear and recorded rates of victimization are by definition
    inadequate and need to be refined. Lagrange (1993) is persuasive on
    this subject.
63 Translator's note: « Peur de victimation » in the original text. See note
    61 above.

A second problem arises in relation to the criminological aspect of this fear. It is easy to understand why fear is associated with a praxic origin: the causal link between crime and fear seems self-evident. Moreover, it is research on deviance that has brought to light the anxiety around the likelihood of victimization. However, such a perspective obscures the fact that anxiety is an awareness constructed from elements external to individual experience but projected onto that experience. The information received about the world external to the self is diffracted by the processing applied to it on its route to emotional experience. The feelings linked to the likelihood of victimization depend on the social context of the actor and her positioning in this context. The whole socio-demographics of collective and individual diversities, from gender and age to neighbourhood, contribute to this diffraction (Box, Hale and Andrews 1988)[64] and there are even plausible hypotheses that see the attitude toward "crime" as a factor in the resistance to change by classes in decline (Robert and Zauberman 1985, Ocqueteau and Perez-Diaz 1989). It is often the least victimized groups that are most afraid, and vice versa (Clemente and Kleiman 1976; Garofolo 1981[65]), a fact whose apparently paradoxical character clarifies the terms of the question and draws attention to the stereotypes of physically violent crime. The construction of the fear of victimization is indeed not based mainly on the experience of being the victim of a

---

64   The close link between perception of the likelihood of victimization and the real rate is so much taken for granted that researchers themselves refer to "anomalies" when survey findings show no inverse relation between socio-economic level and the level of victimization, and speak of "regularities" in the opposite case (Grémy 2000: 174-5).

65   See also Fattah (1981), and Ferraro's objections (1995: 101ff).

violent offence,[66] since such experiences are fairly rare and phobogenic victimization is very strongly concentrated on certain groups and strata (Box 1983). Moreover, the experience of victimization is very often radically different from its imagined projection; in reality, phobogenic crime, when committed, arouses anger.[67] It is, therefore, very important to distinguish between victimization and the fear provoked by its likelihood projected into the future.[68] This differentiation relates directly to the fact that the fear of victimization is largely built on *representations* of "crime" that, in themselves, constitute a distinct theme of the public sphere. News stories on assaults, muggings, burglaries, rapes, or murders make these events the concern of everyone, and for the media, crime consists almost entirely of violent acts between people

---

66 Lagrange and Roché (1987-89) showed that the extent of contact with the social world through one's "network of sociality" (going out, exposure to contact with strangers, etc.) was the best single predictor of fear and also of the likelihood of victimization, i.e. that individuals with the most contacts are more exposed but less worried.

67 It can happen, for example that a reaction of anger overtakes and dispels fear. Jeudy (1979: 62) relates this interesting account of a female victim: "There was someone behind me; I looked round, there was a man following me and not trying to hide it. I could hear his footsteps. I crossed the road to see who it was, and he started to cross too. I kept walking down the middle of the road. He started to assault me sexually at first; I didn't respond. Suddenly he grabbed my bag and ran off. I started to chase him. I was stunned but no longer afraid. I wanted to punch him in the face. He saw me coming toward him and ran off again, and this went on for a long time. Now I think I was crazy to do that, he could have hit me..." Kinsey and Anderson (1992: 60) note that fear during or after the perpetration of the offence is relatively rare. Victims focus much more on the practical problems caused and experience feelings of anger. For similar observations, see van der Wurff and Stringer (1989).

68 Mayhew (1993: 188) presents a series of data that contradict several common perceptions of violent crime. For example, one crime in five involves some kind of violence. In only 1 percent of such crimes is the victim admitted to hospital, which means that only two cases in a thousand involve significant violence (the data come from surveys on victimization and so relate to offences committed and not simply those recorded by the police; they therefore give a much more representative picture of what really happens).

who do not know one another.[69] These messages take several forms, often at the same time: information is mingled with entertainment[70] and sometimes also with the aim of launching public appeals to take precautions or report to the police or testify (such appeals are, more frequent in other western countries than in France). This multiplicity should not be allowed to mask two essential questions. First, the fear of victimization is not built on violent crime but on information about it. So, the relationship between the criminological reality of victimization and the more generally sociological fear of it is distorted by a *double deflection*. On the one hand, there is the distortion of all crimes involved by the receiver of information, according to his or her socio-cognitive context. As with any condition that derives from multiple overlapping stimuli, this deflecting link must be understood as a site of constant, rapid interaction among the senders of the messages and to a lesser extent interaction between them and the receiver. On the other hand, as I already suggested, the problematic of criminogenic insecurity would be better understood if it were integrated into the larger context of the constitution of social threats. If we examine in isolation the problems that relate to a single source, we are less able to understand important and

---

69 Among the three main sources of information influencing fear of victimization (personal experience, the experience of close acquaintances, and the media), "the influence of how the media present deviance on people's view of insecurity is particularly strong; indeed, it is above all TV presentations of urban violence that now most influence opinion in France" (Grémy 1998: 142; see also Schneider 1992: 88; Weaver and Wakshlag 1986).

70 The O. J. Simpson trial in Los Angeles significantly extended the limits of media representations in the realm of phobogenic crime. The story became the biggest national spectacle in US history, and the TV audience (91 percent for the verdict) was greater than for the death of President Kennedy or the first moon landing. The trial not only rivalled Disneyland as an entertainment (*Le Parisien*, February 11-12, 1995) but finally divided public opinion on racial lines.

complex phenomena like xenophobia or exclusion. These are concepts that take for granted social relationships that are not self-evident and whose *dangerizing dimensions and link with normality* can lead to an adequate explanation. The question of defining the marginal automatically brings up the question of constructing the normal, and from the analytical point of view, these two questions only point to two facets of social interaction. Such an approach, therefore, suggests that every social threat should be observed in terms of the mechanisms through which it is constituted. The fear of victimization is thus closely connected with the domain of socio-occupational uncertainty, and this larger problematic is one of the symptoms of probabilistic reasoning, one of the phenomena that arise from post-industrial dangeriza-tion. The overlapping of "social problems" is clearly neither a media invention nor a sociological conclusion, but above all a social reality constantly updated by the cultural order. *If the "inner city or the "banlieue" is the social trash can, this is a condition that is part of its capacity to frighten*, both as a source of threats for the framework of life of those who are outside and as the probable end of a trajectory, triggered by a break in the course of personal or professional life. It is in this more general context that the fear of victimization now takes on its full meaning as a field of dangerization of the experiential world.

IV.1 Suspicion and Atomization: a New "Other"

In the more expensive apartment blocks of those Paris suburbs that are mostly inhabited by the middle class, people regularly find advertisements in their letter boxes from companies offering to install burglar alarms and reinforced doors. On the same day, they can read regular newspaper accounts of incidents involving criminal violence a few miles further north, of the drug gangs who operate there, and the assaults by young people of foreign origin on law-abiding citizens like themselves. The films or series they watch on TV contain on average one act of violence every ten minutes (Cumberbatch 1988: 12).[71] If they read a magazine, they will find an interview with the mayor of a neighbouring town who declares himself highly satisfied with the installation of CCTV cameras on public thoroughfares, which has reduced the number of assaults.[72] Meanwhile, the deputy mayor responsible for security in their municipality offers some advice: among other things, he tells old people not to open the door to callers who claim to represent public bodies, but to demand to see their official credentials or call the police to come and check their status.

This is not a situation peculiar to Paris or to France. On the contrary, similar messages are even more frequent and more structured elsewhere. In their leaflets, the British police urge the public to adopt exactly the same behaviour, showing a shadowy figure on the other side of the door, a security chain and the allusive caption: "*Knock, knock – Who's there?*" While the national administrative paradigm in France appears in the style of advice in contrast with the simple, pragmatic clarity of public discourse in Britain, the idea is the same. The person at the door takes the position of a suspect who must *prove* that he is not lying. It is clearly for this reason that employees of public bodies are provided with identity cards.

---

71   It has been estimated that in the United States in 1988, a young person of average sociodemographic profile had seen 26,000 murders by the age of 18 (*The Observer Magazine*, August 1, 1993).

72   In the early 1990s, the Mayor of Levallois-Perret, Patrick Balkany, proudly announced to the media that his town had installed a CCTV network twice as dense (100 cameras for every 50,000 inhabitants) as in other municipalities in France equipped with such networks (Lambersart, Hénin-Beaumont and Roubaix). CCTV systems are now so common that they are no longer a source of municipal pride.

This climate of growing suspicion is embedded in the
post-industrial way of life. The shadowy figure in the police
leaflets expresses the unusual nature of an unexpected,
unknown visitor at the door, and legitimates immediate
suspicion. The threatening visitor is precisely the bearer
of a random social contact, the point of convergence of
private life with its larger external context, and not with
an institutional context, such as that of employment or
transportation. In other words, the individual in question, the likely aggressor, is very clearly the "absolute
other," lacking the guarantees of an institutional context
which would structure his relationships in advance. The
suspicion that bears on him is generalized. If we place
the message in a praxic model, we can see that some very
important problems arise. The occupant is expected to
continue to regard the visitor as a suspect until she is satisfied that he no longer constitutes a threat.[73] We need to
consider the criteria implicit in this hypothetical filtering.
No one expects a burglar to reply that he has come to
burgle or to prepare to do so; an "aggressor" (a term that
incidentally reflects no precise offence but only the fear of
victimization[74]) looks, in principle, no more suspect than
the next-door neighbour. On the contrary, it is clear that a
probable offender will offer an excuse that is as banal and

---

73 It is important to note that things are supposed to unfold in this way, even
    in a country whose citizens still enjoy the right not to have to prove their
    identity. Personal identity cards do not exist in Great Britain. Conservative
    discourse on crime has sought to take advantage of a "European" format
    of driving license to introduce the photograph of its holder and then
    move to an obligatory identity card; this project has been widely seen
    as a potential infringement of public freedom (*The Guardian*, August
    22, 1994). The topic regularly crops up as a major question in British
    political life and public discussion. When the debate started in 1990, 37
    percent of the population was in favour of obligatory identity cards while
    40 percent opposed them (Jowell et al. 1991: 182-3).

74 Translator's note: The term « agresseur » is used in French to mean a
    very broad range of unwanted, harassing, or dangerous behaviours.

plausible as that of someone who is not lying; the simulation of "normal" behaviour is part of the offence. In reality, the individual confronted with these circumstances has no basis for making an effective choice in order to detect and avert the danger. The function of the precautionary security message thus acquires another dimension. One could opt either for a systematic refusal of contact with others in these circumstances, or for a "filtering" approach based on a profile constructed on preconceptions and reinforced through repetition (xenophobic attitudes, fear of young people, etc.).[75] The notion of the suspect as such both condenses and externalizes a set of probabilistic and, for the most part, arbitrary judgments about the "other" invariably dangerized as an offender. Beyond the reproduction of preconceived schemas, the organization of the fear of victimization around suspicion corrodes the mechanisms of confidence in the social bond and thus deepens the polarization of the wider society around relationships ever more determined by their institutional context. However, the context of dangerization of others constitutes at the same time one of the reasons but also a general consequence of atomizing tendencies and contributes decisively to their self-proliferation.

In the situation above, for example, the precautionary message places the individual, with mathematical certainty, in an intractable bind.[76] However, this would be

---

75 It is difficult to contradict Taguieff (1991: 192) when he observes that "nowadays [in France] the fear of the Other is preferentially focused on the 'Muslim immigrant.'" On the implications of the cultural diversities relating exclusively to the fear of victimization, see Covington and Taylor (1991).

76 Not surprisingly, "the evidence reviewed strongly suggests that crime prevention advertising has, in itself, failed to produce changes in the behaviour of potential victims and offenders," as Riley and Mayhew (1980: 1-2) point out, not forgetting to explain that: "Apart from its obvious purpose of reducing crime rates, such advertising is seen as valuable in showing official concern about crime."

a neutral act if it did not emphasize the threat carried by the external world. The possibility or the impasse that the individual decision embodies is part of risk management in private life, just as much as the dangerization of others refers to the representation of society as a whole for each actor. This bifurcation, linked to the probability of becoming a victim, means that the threat is realized as much as a category of individual experience as a factor of communication in society. In practical terms, not opening one's door means regarding as normal a world where no one opens his door to anyone. In the last 30 or 40 years, this self-evidence has become established as a neutral practice, since everything outside the totally and exclusively controlled environment (house, shop, car, office, or workplace) is deeply dangerized. Manufacturers and installers offer reinforced doors, the police provide free security assessments, and private security firms enjoy spectacular growth in their business (Ocqueteau 1992). Crime takes the form of another enemy of society. The spirit of "beating crime together"[77] expresses the embarrassment that late modernity senses before its criminogenic necessity. It transforms the phobogenic criminal act into a notion comprehensible through its demonization and compatible with political governance. As Cohen (1971: 10) observes: "We can only know what it is to be saintly by being told just what the shape of the devil is." Thus, fear becomes the reverse image of compliance, and dangerization is coupled with regularization.

Before us unfolds the schema of perioptic sociality. The "other" is delegitimated and banished from the expe-

---

77   This was the slogan of a long and extensive publicity campaign by the police in the United Kingdom. It invites comparison with the slogan "watchful together," seen everywhere in the Paris public transportation system after the attacks in the Regional Express network (RER) in the mid-1990s.

riential world when she cannot display a precise function or role; delegitimated as an individual presence, as "the other," and not as "the public" or "people" or some other collective existence belonging to the order of the imaginary or the cultural. The fear of victimization is both generated in and reinforces a more general dynamics of atomization. However, we know nothing of the mechanisms that link this fear to the model of society within which it develops. The plausible hypothesis that this link exists sheds no light on the real questions. Social phenomena do not recognize the distinction between causality and the way things come into being, forming and being formed are two facets of a single reality. Thus, our real problem is to know what factors cause the fear of victimization to infiltrate the social body, and how they generate this dynamics of dangerization of the "other."

IV.2 Public Sphere

What is called "safety" in the public sphere is an aspect of social reality that is attracting increasing interest, and in new ways. "Crime," as a generalized fear, occupies a truly central and durable place in contemporary societies. Levels of anxiety rise constantly. In the United States, a society whose values and principles of organization have gained particular significance in the post-industrial epoch, "crime" is the major pole of anxiety. In the 1990s in both Britain and France it was also considered the most important problem after unemployment.[78] Two inseparably intertwined fields are very clearly linked to this rise in

---

78   For a comparative aspect, see Kegels (1982). In France, 52 percent of the population rank "growing insecurity" as the most preoccupying question, second only to unemployment; insecurity is far ahead of "maintaining purchasing power" (28 percent) (Roché 1993: 80). In Great Britain, crime was similarly ranked as the second most important problem after unemployment, ahead of "the economic situation" (MORI poll, *Public Attitudes to Crime*, January 1994).

anxiety, although this does not necessarily mean that they
have provoked it: media messages[79] and political discourse.
I introduce here a bifurcation to present some interesting
points from two approaches embedded in different
cultural contexts. These parallel references reveal that the
dangerization of the social bond is a structural tendency of
late modernity, since it emerges as much in the structures
of the liberal sociality associated with the "Anglo-Saxon"
countries as in republican societies inspired by the imaginary projection of egalitarian solidarity. The conception
of the "other" and the place reserved for him, his rights
to difference, and his obligations of assimilation are mark-
edly different in France and Britain;[80] but the "other's"
erosion by suspicion and the sense of vulnerability that he
generates are much more similar.

IV.3 Britain: the Right to Difference and Penal Populism

The consumption of images of violence is solidly
anchored in Britain, and the domination of the media
by the threat of victimization is strongly established. It
is characteristic that, in a country whose broadcasting
has served as a model for the world, where the televisual
media are not only regulated but also self-monitored,
and where the penalties for media offences are high,
56 percent of prime-time fiction consists of programs
containing violent acts.[81] In the press, the daily reports
of the tabloids emphasize the bloodshed in any event,
while the "quality papers" give generous coverage to

79   Studies of this link confirm a strong correlation. Last and Jackson (in
     Williams and Dickinson 1993: 35) report that 70 percent of their respon-
     dents attributed their awareness of the risk of victimization to the media.
80   I avoid here speaking of the United Kingdom as a whole, since Northern
     Ireland is a space with a very different relation to phobogenic offences.
81   The percentages for Japan and the United States are 81 and 80, respec-
     tively (Cumberbatch 1988: 12).

the alarming growth in the crime figures and inner-city jungles. Little importance seems to be attached to plausible doubts, such as the fact that the rise in the number of incidents reported to the police is linked to insurance claims or that social changes give more opportunities for the reporting of crimes committed within the family or among close acquaintances, such as domestic violence, child abuse, or rape.[82] The fact that a large proportion of offences are linked to car theft or driving does not seem in any way to reduce the fear of violence to the person. The emphasis is always on offences involving physical violence with serious consequences, and especially, of course, murder. Because the public sphere in Britain enjoys a tradition combining the absence of generalizing declarations with the examination of details that would not arouse public interest elsewhere,[83] one might suppose that the positions of the political parties would be more nuanced than in other countries. However, their messages in the media are oriented toward a never-ending competition for the role of protector of the public against wrong-doers. The "tough on crime" model continues to hold sway even if "third-way" New Labour also promised to be "tough on the causes of crime." This model very often signifies much harsher sentences, which are intended to prove the government's intention to "fight crime" (Loveday 1994: 188-190; see also Glaster 1992: 14ff). Held hostage by a direct association between phobogenic crime and imprisonment, the government

---

82 Televised representations of acts of violence, following the persistent model of the unknown assailant from outside is one of the most common distortions of the offences committed. For viewers of American productions throughout the world, it is hard to believe that 85 percent of murders in the United States are committed within the family circle (Katz and Vesin 1986: 21).

83 As, for example, on the question of equipping the police with American-style batons or firearms (*The Scotsman*, May 17, 1994).

thus asserts its control over society and at the same time
seeks to reassure the citizens that it is still reasonably safe
to move about freely. The fight against crime is, to some
extent, a product of the negative consequences that
publicizing "criminality" can have, such as effects on the
real estate market or tourism. It is also the temporary
and embarrassed response to the fear of victimization.
Thus, violent crime is increasingly the front-page story.[84]
The competition among the political parties and also
within the media continues to grow, to the point of being
identified as a distinct and permanent phenomenon of
the public sphere, recently named "penal populism."[85]

The question is increasingly posed in the context of
a social threat. Several widely reported cases form the
epitome of the dangerousness of the young male from
a poor background.[86] Operation Eagle Eye, launched
by the Metropolitan Police of Greater London in the
summer of 1995, institutionalized this approach by
recommending particular vigilance toward young black
males (*The Times*, July 29 and August 4, 1995). The
strongly criticized behaviour of the police in the death
of Stephen Lawrence, a black teenager murdered by a
group of racist youths, subsequently showed the extent
of racial prejudice in the police force. An independent
inquiry into the actions of the police acknowledged the
existence of "institutional racism" in the police, opening
a new chapter in the social relations of the country. In
psychological terms, one of the cases most projected by

---

84 As shown, for example, by the media reaction to the murder of the jour-
    nalist Jill Dando on April 26, 1999.
85 For a detailed history of the rise of this phenomenon, see Nash (1999:
    33 ff).
86 One example was the case of Michael Carling, Mayor of Tickhill in South
    Yorkshire, who "suffered serious head injuries and a broken jaw after he
    tried to stop a gang of youths trampling a flower-bed" (*The Independent*,
    July 10, 1995).

the British and European media in recent years was the murder of James Bulger, where the context was substantially different (the victim was aged just under three, and the two offenders were ten). The medio-political discourse, however, followed the usual lines of a society in which everyone is subject to the risk of victimization. The Home Secretary called the two children "two nasty pieces of work" and exercised his right to increase their sentences to the maximum possible (*The Daily Telegraph*, February 22, 1996).

IV.4 The Image

In Britain, violent crime is present in the media in a way not seen in France.[87] In particular, the reconstruction of violent offences is set in a context of "helping with inquiries" in the monthly program *Crimewatch UK*, which started in 1984.[88] This is a "reality TV" show that aims to present and reconstruct phobogenic crimes without adding elements that would make its presentation overtly sensational (music, fast editing, close-ups, etc.). The legitimation of this presentation lies in the fact that viewers can see in detail where and how a crime took place in order to assist the police in solving it. Items of evidence, images from CCTV cameras, and photofits are also shown, and viewers are invited to phone the studio, where police officers await their information. The

---

87 The occasional program *Témoin Numéro 1* ("First Witness") on the French TV channel TF1 a few years ago was more a summary compiled for entertainment than a precise approach to the events involved.

88 The format was inspired by the occasional German TV program *Aktenzeichen XY…Ungelöst* ("Case XY… Unsolved"), which started in 1967 and was used as a media tool by the police, mainly oriented toward politically motivated crime and especially the Baader-Meinhof group. *Crimewatch UK* does not focus systematically on "ideologically motivated" offences linked to the IRA. For a critical and comparative presentation of the program, see Schlesinger and Tumber (1993).

program's contribution to crime solving is repeatedly
highlighted. It has attracted a certain amount of attention from criminologists and media specialists, because
the association between such a show and the fear of
victimization is at least a legitimate hypothesis.

Crimewatch UK attracts "[...] more viewers than
some popular TV series, and [...] many more than the
main evening news" – 9 to 13 million, with no sign of
decline – and it enjoys a very high viewer appreciation
rating (Schlesinger, Tumber and Murdock 1991:407;
Schlesinger and Tumber 1993: 19, 22-3). This phenomenon is in itself a social development. It is not necessary
to explain the media realism around crime in order to
testify to these results.[89] Moreover, this realism moves in
a limited context. The broader media landscape main-
tains its long tradition of making investigations while
avoiding sensational elements, and a significant part of
the public responds to this know-how.[90] The program
therefore emphasizes the presentation of the facts and
the search for the suspects, and not the condemnation
or demonization of offenders.

This model of cultural treatment of danger, in
contrast to a model of risk management, touches on
phobogenic crime actively, i.e. by presenting the source
of fear in connection with an action plan. Victimization
is thus diffused as an event and a probability that the
viewer can do something about – contribute to the arrest
of the offenders and be aware of safety issues. What these
two roles have in common is the investigative gaze on
reality: "If you know someone who looks like this picture

---

89 A first consequence, which often escapes criminological critique, is that
    the media treatment of crime plays a crucial role in the definition of
    deviance (Carriere and Ericson 1989).
90 There are several investigative programs with different themes, such as
    Panorama or *Dispatches*, which observe certain standards of quality.

and who might have been at the scene of the crime... if you know anything about this person... or if you saw someone use this ...," are questions that bear on the investigation of an offence already committed, but also touch on the probability that such a grave offence is reproducible and can therefore affect *every* viewer. The crucial importance of the generalized awareness of this probability is not fully apparent without considering the factors necessary for fear to arise. It is only when there is the perception of a *high* probability of victimization through a *serious* offence that fear of victimization becomes possible (Warr and Stafford 1983).

The prescribed reaction to the danger of victimization is to *examine* the world of experience from a police point of view and reveal its danger content. Precaution also consists in first examining the lived experience from the point of view of a potential victim as if one were already the target of a "criminal." Scrutinizing the media to verify the *similarity* between the environment where the offence took place and one's own environment is both a reaction of legitimate interest and a factor tending to increase one's fear.[91] Every message "against crime," in fact, contains a comparative reference to the social world. Its diffusion neutralizes in practice the low probability of victimization and works to induce in the actor another autoscopic point of view, another threatening facet of reality that competes with other threats to establish its comparative importance in the consciousness of the viewer.

---

91   There is a close relationship between the viewer's fear and the param-
     eters relating the viewer to the victim and her environment (Winkel and
     Vrij 1990). It has also been found that the degree of difference between
     the place of the offence and the environment of the viewer, listener, or
     reader leads to a sense of "comparative safety" (Liska and Baccaglini
     1990). Calculation of sociodemographic proximity to the victim does not
     reduce general fear; it simply 'refines' it while involving the subject in
     ever higher awareness of a dangerous world.

IV.5 Vigilance

Such a degree of dangerization naturally leads to large-scale reactive initiatives. One of these is the archipelago of units of surveillance and precaution "against crime" based on the local area and known as Neighbourhood Watch Schemes (NWS). Their proliferation has shown how much they corresponded to the real anxieties of the population.[92] Each NWS is set up by the police, who approach the population of the neighbourhood to encourage a meeting of a group of residents who may be concerned about preventing offences and prepared to act in the framework of the scheme. There is a group coordinator for each street in the neighbourhood and a scheme coordinator who has a permanent link with a designated police officer. The aim of the NWS is to "give the police the extra eyes and ears they need to fight the ever-growing [*sic*] level of crime." Each member is invited among other things "to be on the alert for crime or suspicious situations that could lead to a crime being committed" (*Neighbourhood Watch Handbook*). For each group of residents, a designated police officer provides liaison and advises on security, safety, and precautionary issues. Because of the independence of regional police forces in Britain (Jones, Newburn and Smith 1994: 12-16),[93] the role of each NWS can vary. In general, the police disapprove of interventionist approaches on the part of members (for example, patrols, accosting suspects, etc.) and an attempt by the Home Secretary to introduce voluntary patrols by NWS members failed, having been resisted as much by the police as by scheme coordinators

---

92 In early 1988, 14 percent of British households belonged to existing schemes and two thirds of those that did not were prepared to join if a scheme were set up in their neighbourhoods (Mayhew, Elliott and Dowds 1989: 64).

93 The British model of policing is also quite opposed to the centralized, "authoritarian" approach of continental countries (Monjardet 1993).

(*The Independent*, August 16, 1994). What is asked of each member is to be aware of "safety" in his neighbourhood, to inform the police of anything "suspicious," and to discuss the pattern of offences and the appropriate preventive tactics at the members' meetings. The NWS encourages its members to tactically improve their personal and domestic security and that of their neighbourhoods. In practice, this precautionary approach permeates not only neighbourhood life but also the private space of the person. Residents should mark their possessions with an ultraviolet pen and engrave their postcode on their domestic appliances and car windows so that their origin will always be recognizable in the event of theft. Before going on holiday, they should inform their neighbours, and they can put a sticker, provided by the scheme, on their letterboxes so that junk mail does not accumulate and attract attention. Above all, one should display on one's windows that one belongs to the NWS; signs are also fixed to lampposts in the street to indicate that "This is a Neighbourhood Watch Area," to deter possible offenders. As can readily be supposed, the NWS is implicitly a *de facto* attempt to recreate links between the inhabitants of the neighbourhood, since it not only sets up regular contact for the exchange of information, but also defines the responsibility of each toward the others.

Although the initiative was introduced by the police to improve the situation in "tough" neighbourhoods, several studies have shown that it was better suited to lower-middle and middle-class neighbourhoods (Mayhew, Elliott and Dowds 1989: 53; Jones, Newburn and Smith 1994: 104). This seems to be explained by the fact that a combination of two factors is required to ensure lasting participation: on the one hand, fear of victimization and, on the other, a strong sense of social cohesion (Bennett 1989). Seen from an angle that takes account of the relationship between the actor and the dangerization of his experiential world, this is hardly surprising. What the data confirm is that participation in the scheme depends more on an active reaction to fear of victimization than on the rate of offences in the neighbourhood (Hope 1988).[94] Although the propagation of "anti-social behaviour" in housing estates, where low incomes are concentrated explains in part the relative failure of a strongly participative structure, other reasons contribute as well, such as the lack of architectural infrastructure[95] or the fact that attachment to law and order and the fear of victimization are higher among those who from several points of view are less likely to become victims. In other words, the lack of contact with danger aggravates fear. The involvement of residents in NWSs predictably shows that those who feel they have something important to protect are more likely to mobilize as a consequence of their suspicion of others. The dangers thought to threaten the life of the neighbourhood vary according to the context. People in a lower-middle-class neighbourhood will get involved in their NWS because of vandalism by young people from adjacent "tough" areas, while those in a comfortable middle-class neighbourhood, with no problems of vandalism or violence, will focus their anxiety on disturbances from the local pub.

The NWS is an interesting structure in several ways. As an organization, it is a rare example of a supposedly "'spontaneous'" community (a "neighbourhood") assembled around an institution (the police). As an action project, it consists of putting the community on alert; it

---

94 On participation in similar schemes in the United States, see Lavrakas and Hertz (1982) and Skogan (1982).

95 Poorly lit areas are systematically seen as places where crimes are committed, regardless of the rates actually recorded (Vrij and Winkel 1991).

institutionalizes (and therefore, to some extent, invents) a
phobogenic content for the reality of the neighbourhood
and its inhabitants. Even more, it tactically prepares the
neighbourhood for a possible "attack" by offenders or
delinquents by trying to reduce their gains and increase
their risks. One of the functions of these schemes is to separate the residents from "outsiders." Yanay (1994: 53) notes
that "the definition of outsiders is personal. Outsiders are
all those people who either do not look familiar [...] or
who do not look as if they live in the community or belong
to it." It is, therefore, not surprising that 44 percent of
the coordinators of the groups studied take different positions on reporting incidents to the police, depending on
whether or not an "outsider" is involved. At another level,
the message the NWS seems to send to this outsider is
simple: the scheme displays its own existence.[96] But the
content of this message is long and varied, because it
condenses the totality of the functions of the scheme that
are projected toward members, non-members, habitual
users, and occasional visitors — and sometimes, perhaps,
toward someone who is planning an offence.

What is the cement that binds such diverse elements
together in a structure? How does the viewer become
an investigator, an accident or crime a form of entertainment, the neighbourhood a policing concept? What
allows the development of *CrimewatchUK* or NWSs – such
unprecedented, "multi-structures," in the sense that they
combine previously unconnected means toward the same
goal? While a large part of the fear of victimization can be
attributed to the media, it also has to be acknowledged
that the broadcasting media use violent crime to keep and
increase their viewing figures *because* the public reacts with

---

96   "*Neighbourhood Watch* has made more of an impact, in terms of visibility
if nothing else, than any other community crime prevention effort in
Britain" (Mayhew, Elliott and Dowds 1989: 51).

more interest in this area. Erickson (1991: 221) rightly observes that "the mass media are not unambiguous entities; they are ascribed meaning by their users." Although the domain of representation of crime is much more an artefact than a reflection of the experiential world, *the authenticity of concerns about the danger of crime remains unaffected.* A number of institutional actors seek to "mobilize" the population around a particular focus, but only *some* of them achieve their aim, and only for *a part* of society. The relationship between the institutional structure and its user is indeed subject to a series of factors that influence not only the reason *why* people choose to follow this or that message, but also *what* people "see" in the chosen message.[97] A program on violent crime, a report on poor neighbourhoods, and a sign announcing the existence of an NWS are all integrated in a viewpoint in which "crime" is almost asocial, an evil against which one must defend oneself, a phenomenon outside the limits of society that may concern everyone, but only as a potential victim. Crime seen as a threat dominates the public sphere, and the individual focus is displaced toward anxiety and defensive strategies. If *Crimewatch UK* and NWSs prove one thing, it is that it is possible to place phobogenic crime at the centre of a society without recognizing in it any other dimension than that of a praxic problem. The constitution of a social condition as a threat thus offers a new territory for the radicalization of the liberal model. By exploiting fear of victimization as a personal event, it becomes possible for the institutional actors to assert that the only conceivable solution regarding deviance is to try to develop individual defensive strategies and devices.

---

97   In the most common conditions, the viewer chooses programs that confirm opinions he already holds (Gunter 1987: 97ff). Moreover, it is also pertinent to note that ideological and sociocognitive differentiations lead to distinct models of fear of crime (Parker 1988).

IV.6 France: "Integration" and Silent Dangerization

The different conception of the danger of victimization in France corresponds to the different model of governance around the Republic. The centralization of the administration and the model of the mediation of power through the state, and not only through managerial administration, contribute, among other factors, to the understanding of deviance as a challenge to the founding principles of the socio-political system. Violent crime is presented in the media as a threat to public order, an act to be condemned but not a problem to be solved. Thus, deviance is the concern of the state, a social phenomenon that must be contained or even eradicated by a police force that has no autonomy with respect to the government. The type of crime that creates a safety panic is one that throws down a challenge to the order established by the Republic. The unfolding of a relatively recent offence of this kind exemplifies this model of reaction. It was committed in October 1994 by two young people whom the media dubbed "the Vincennes couple." Three policemen, a taxi driver, and one of the offenders were killed in a car chase that resulted from a police decision to violently confront the offenders in an open public space. The action on the part of the police practically caused at least two of the deaths. Yet, the media accounts hardly criticized the police operation, which was so incompetent that it led to gross errors, such as shooting at a car driven by a hostage.[98] In such cases, the threat is seen as an assault on the Republic and the national community that identifies with

---

98   For the hostage's account, see *VSD*, N° 893, October 13, 1994; for the media reaction, see *Le Monde*, October 7, 1994.

it.[99] By contrast, cases involving crimes between private individuals, not implying a direct confrontation with the state, provide minor news items that rarely reach the front page. Dangerization, directed in this context more toward imaginary principles than concrete applications, easily casts its shadow on whole sectors of the population and remains exclusively attached to the domains of order and citizenship, while skirting around the social problems that surround the source of the threat.

Moreover, the state itself, especially in the hands of a conservative government, will sometimes launch a safety panic. The repeated security operations under the Balladur government were indeed only a "spectacle" (*Libération*, August 11, 1994). Random checks on cars entering Paris and other cities, daily identity checks on people belonging to ethnic and racial minorities in railway stations and the subway, body searches for no particular reason, do not merely display the message of a government "fighting crime";[100] they confirm in the most visible way that there is indeed a threat to the security of French society. Moreover, it demonstrates a threat so grave that the country has to be put on a high state of alert by institutional security mechanisms.[101] The

---

99   The hostage-taking by Erick Schmitt in a kindergarten in Neuilly in May 1994 is an example of this symbolism. The ministerial version was largely accepted and relayed by the media. Doubts arose later as to the need to "neutralize" the hostage-taker, since he was very probably shot while asleep (Patrie and Vogelweith 1994).

100 For a discussion of the practice of giving "symbolic reassurance" through police visibility, see Henig and Maxfield (1978). On the problems of the management of crime by the political authorities in France, see Robert (1985).

101 The same model was applied after the bomb attack in the Paris suburban train network on July 25, 1995. The first measures taken were to close the borders opened under the Schengen Agreement and step up identity checks; the threat was systematically presented as coming "from outside" (*Le Monde,* June 27, 1995).

fear of victimization is largely based on a silent xenophobia, since membership of the Republic prevents
public, and often private, debate on the relationship
between the dangerized "other" and the perception of
ethnic and racial minorities. This relationship develops
at the level of individual consciousness and private
networks, without reference to external elements such
as the offences attributed to minorities (Roché 1993:
233ff). For the individual actor, this context is inevitably
represented as governed in a top-down manner. The
precautionary role of the individual is thus confined to
measures for the atomized, independent improvement
of her own safety. The fear of victimization operates
both at the level of the threat for the wider society as
an imaginary reference and at the strictly atomized
level of the individual as a reference to the praxic
world. This split, which excludes the possibility of an
active, collective sharing of the threatening projections,
structures the fear of victimization around institutional
actors (the state, the police, the justice system, security
firms, etc.) without offering a margin for the management of fear through intersubjective communication.[102]
This model thus reproduces and reinforces the
perioptic nature of the perception of deviant dangerousness and the resulting social inertia. There is no
dynamics aimed at establishing a relationship between
the public sphere and experience on local terrain, so
as to make the threat of victimization more concrete
and rational. The absence of such a dynamics can be
observed in several features that include: (a) the strong
growth in corporate use of private security services;

---

102 On management of the fear of victimization by the state in France, see
  Roché (1993: 85-100).

(b) the rising demand for domestic security equipment,[103] (c) the absence of socio-media relations and media-political messages concerning the reduction of phobogenic crimes; and (d) the absence of non-governmental institutions and organizations concerned with reducing victimization, with the relationship between society and the offender, or with questions of social and ethnic stratification among offenders and victims.

The construction of dangerized "others" in France makes it impossible to discuss their difference and, therefore, the way they are perceived. In total contrast with British cultural liberalism, the public projection of the threat is here confined by the sense of a theoretically egalitarian citizenship. This results in a radicalization of ethnic relations, represented as much by the social segregation of minorities as by a political and social discourse that unequivocally professes "integration" without ever thinking of the dominating rejection of the unassimilated that it expresses. This facilitates the legitimation of a perception of "others" (social, ethnic, or sexual) that silently excludes them. Precautions and strategies against victimization are therefore deployed not on the hypothesis that one should avoid crime, but on the premise that

---

103 On the state's loss of control over safety unrelated to public order, see Ocqueteau (1995, 1990). In numerical terms, in the early 1990s there were almost two private security guards for every three police officers (Nenquin 1993: 161-2); By 1988, one in three large retail firms were using CCTV systems against shop-lifting and robbery, and one in two had security guards (Ocqueteau 1992). This tendency is set in a more general context of social organization. By as early as 1972, almost $5 billion of the $12 billion spent on security services in the United States concerned the private sector (Kakalik and Wildhorn 1977). Moreover, the endeavour to close the gap in status between private and public security actors is developing in several countries at the highest level of organizational confluence, with a growing number of senior police officers moving to private security companies that aspire to "police" status (*The Independent on Sunday*, May 23, 1993).

one should avoid the perpetrator. The egalitarian façade makes this marginalization possible as a private option, an extraordinary coincidence of individual decisions, rather than a sustainable principle of social and economic life. It is true that the potential in terms of social justice, and, therefore, of less biased perception, is more important here than in a context that concentrates on individual merit; but it is also true that fear of others can more easily develop in an arbitrary and, therefore, uncontrollable way.

IV.7 Private Fortification

The diversity in the structuring of the dangerization of others concerns above all the channels through which fear is distributed and its public projections. This diversity lies in the socio-historical differences produced or espoused by modernity in its development in different countries. It would be a mistake to ignore these differences both in the construction of the "other" and more generally in the construction of the social. It is precisely these differences that confirm the advent of a new stage in homogenization, which is very pronounced in the new control, its causes, and its impacts. While the configuration of social perceptions still allows the existence of formations different from those just described, the convergence of recent shared tendencies confirms that the influence of the post-industrial conjuncture transcends national differences and unites them in a new paradigm, dangerizing social spaces in a similar way despite cultural specificities. The importance of this paradigm is as great as its capacity to saturate practices, strategies, and perceptions vis-à-vis the "other" in a way that can be recognized throughout the industrial world.

At the origin of this defensive wisdom lies globalized interaction and the technological and discursive similarity of thematically specialized structures. The control measures taken are often designed to be identical, because they have to be compatible. So, everywhere in the world a bank card is associated with a code, the identification of a person is associated with fingerprints,[104] and funds are transported in armoured vehicles. The development of preliminary inspection devices by private institutions eliminates the understanding of crime as a social problem. The regression of intersubjective evaluation of the acts of others and its replacement by the issuing of institutional "standards" leads to the evaporation of moral judgement in favour of risk assessment. The problem, cast in terms of private life, is not to manage phobogenic crime as a social phenomenon, but to manage *one's own likelihood* of victimization. The issue is, therefore, neither to challenge others nor to rely on them,[105] but to escape the probability of victimization.

This explains why such a high proportion of individuals, and more especially women, are adopting precautionary strategies against their potential victimization,[106] at an ever-growing rate (see table below; also Skogan 1986). We also know that, in Europe, in some of the poorest neighbourhoods half the population simply does not go out after dusk (Loveday 1994:

---

104 Since April 9, 1995, this has no longer been exclusively the case. Great Britain now has a national DNA database, the first of its kind in the world. The police have the right to take a hair from suspects and offenders and compare it with the database.

105 Interest in the long series of cases of non-assistance in urban environments started with the murder of Kitty Genovese in New York in 1964, which was witnessed by several people who did not intervene and did not call the police, assuming that "someone else" had done so (Feldman 1993: 413ff).

106 Anecdotally it can be noted that an inflatable doll recently became available on the market, for women who drive alone. Shaped like a muscular man, the doll rides in the passenger seat to deter "would-be carjackers." It is also recommended that the driver talk to it to make the situation look more credible. The inflatable man, called "Safety," has been commercially successful in the United States.

189). Ferraro found that: "Most respondents prefer to avoid danger rather than try to work their way out of it. Yet, there are a variety of ways to avoid danger. Most Americans try to steer clear of 'trouble' but also feel they need to equip themselves and their homes for various contingencies in a world rife with victimization risk" (Ferraro 1995: 115; see also Skogan 1986).[107] In Britain, 79 percent of the population (86 percent of women) avoid "certain types of individuals, as a precaution against crime" (Hough 1995: 65). There is no reason to think that the situation is different in France, although there are no precise data on the avoidance of categories of persons.[108] It seems a plausible hypothesis, which the data tend to support, that the perception of the likelihood of victimization is itself intensified by recourse to precautionary strategies. If fear provokes precaution, precaution provokes more fear and leads the individual deeper into security-related atomization: "the higher one's perceived risk, the more he or she has constrained everyday activities; and the more the person constrains everyday activities, the more he or she will be afraid of crime" (Ferraro 1995: 63; see also Ackermann, Dulong and Jeudy 1983: 15). Such risk-reduction strategies should not be seen as exceptional. They are being integrated into a lifestyle that is accordingly transformed and giving rise to a new normality in which protecting oneself becomes paramount. A panoply of high-tech security devices is already available to the individual user. Often, these are systems that amalgamate all threats by offering an overall response to all the different types of danger that could threaten the individual. A computerized home-security system

---

107   For the distribution of fear after violent incidents and reactions in terms of possession of weapons, see Archer and Erlich-Erfer (1991).

108   For some indices of this tendency, see Lagrange (2000).

can include smoke detectors that call the fire brigade, presence detectors that call the police, and atmospheric pollution sensors that activate household air-purification devices.[109]

Graph 2: Defensive and Avoidance Bahaviours, USA

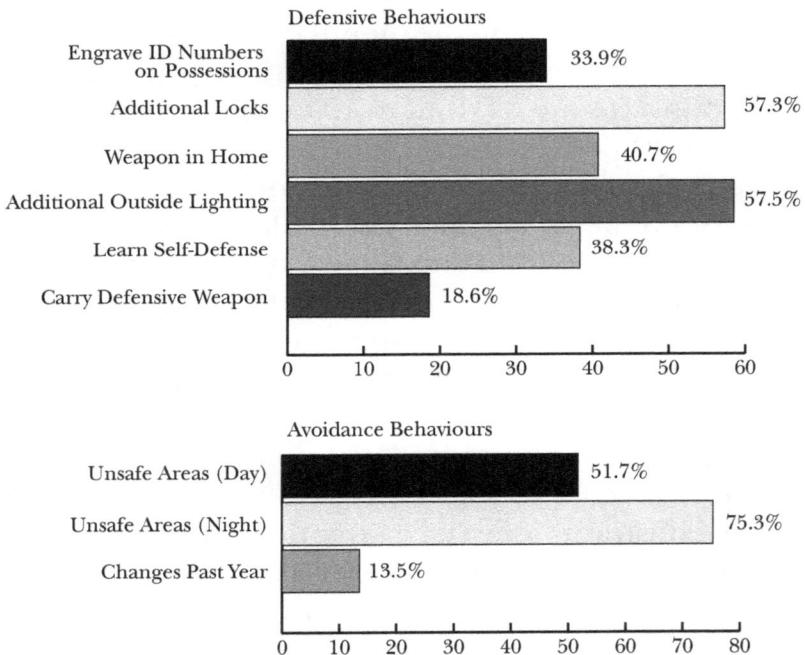

Defensive Behaviours

Behaviour	Value
Engrave ID Numbers on Possessions	33.9%
Additional Locks	57.3%
Weapon in Home	40.7%
Additional Outside Lighting	57.5%
Learn Self-Defense	38.3%
Carry Defensive Weapon	18.6%

Avoidance Behaviours

Behaviour	Value
Unsafe Areas (Day)	51.7%
Unsafe Areas (Night)	75.3%
Changes Past Year	13.5%

Source: Kevin F. Ferraro 1995. Fear of Crime:
Interpreting Victimization Risk (SUNY Press)

This integrated, growing, solitary management of multiple dangers also is also represented at the level of criminological theory and concrete legislation. Penal policies that treat offenders according to their supposed dangerousness are being put in place. The "selective incapacitation" model favours a policy of imprisonment for

---

109   For an overview of domestic security systems, see Miles (1988: 109-11).

offenders with a "high risk" of recidivism (Bottoms 1983).[110]
A new actuarial justice is emerging, aiming at the preemp-
tive neutralization of potential offenders. A person is
punished not for the crime that he has already committed
but for the phobogenic crime that he is likely to commit,
in the view of "experts" (Feeley and Simon 1994). This
approach not only punishes on the basis of offences not yet
committed but reinvents the wheel by excluding the social
perspective on deviant behaviour: attributes such as young,
poorly educated, drug-addicted, little or no employment
history, naturally lead to a high-risk profile. In reality, this
approach thus masks social problems by representing them
as problems of actuarial calculation in a strictly utilitarian
approach to crime. This model is part of the larger paradigm of the treatment of "dangerousness". Castel (1991:
147) observes with reference to its applications in the
psychiatric milieu that "in terms of logic, the diagnosis of
dangerousness collapses the category of the possible onto
that of the real, on the grounds that the possible is more
or less probable". Deviance is thus suppressed as a domain
of the social, to reappear as a grid for punitive evaluation,
stripped of considerations of social stratification except as
regards its utility for the "low-risk" classes.

Symmetrical with this penological approach is the "situational" prevention of crime, which treats the reduction of
offences as a technical, tactical domain (Clarke 1992). The
social dimension of the offences involved is of no interest
to this paradigm, which does not aim either to explain or
to analyze their emergence. The model seeks to prevent
offences through the use of devices put in place by the

---

110 See also *Criminologie* Vol. XVII, N° 2, 1984, devoted to dangerousness.
The problems raised by the evaluation of criminal dangerousness relate
not only to the missing sociological dimensions, but also to the technical
reliability of the approach, where very high margins of predictive error
have been observed (Reiss 1992).

potential victims, and it is synonymous with "target hardening," i.e. measures making it more difficult to commit
the offence, such as installing alarms, video cameras, access
control devices, etc. The success of the approach, in narrow
terms of avoiding victimization, is indisputable.[111] It is seen in
the reduced rate of thefts from houses with burglar alarms
or of cars equipped with theft alarms. However, critics have
already pointed out that these results should be seen as
relative. A central question that arises with respect to this
atomized fortification concerns its consequences for "non-
hardened" targets. The displacement of offences toward the
less protected,[112] as an expression of the stratified distribution
of risks, has been the subject of theoretical propositions for
action aimed at a more equitable distribution of victimization ("crime deflection") (Barr and Pease 1990).

This hypothesis can and should be seen as a facet
of the general problematic of the social distribution of
risk. Mary Douglas (1986: 14-15) sets out four models of
thinking about risk in terms of social justice: "risk pool,"

---

111 It is characteristic, for example, that among the 68 tasks listed in the legal
"job description" of Crime Prevention Officers in England, "the bulk of
the work was concerned with target hardening, surveillance, entry/exit
screening and access control – all standard techniques of 'situational
prevention'" (Jones, Newburn, and Smith 1994: 52-3).

112 The management of these displacements is becoming a priority for local
authorities: "One year ago barely a handful of councils were considering
installing cameras. Now more than 300 are planning to do so, including
Perth, a green-wellie and Barbour town with a low crime rate. Nearby
Stirling and Dundee are installing systems, and Perth says it does not
want their displaced crime" (*The Independent*, July 6, 1994). In terms of
individual protection, one should not underestimate the influence of
the strategy of insurance companies, which offer rebates to householders
with security equipment or make protection measures a condition of
coverage (Ocqueteau 1995). This policy factor significantly accelerates
the concentration of phobogenic offences on sectors of the population
that cannot afford the cost of insurance, much less that of the equipment
required.

cost-benefit analysis, egalitarianism, and the libertarian ethical system. Beck (1995) shows that the distribution of non-global "ecological" risks follows and reproduces the lines of social stratification. Another theoretical current makes the redistribution of industrial risks one of the central factors in redressing the social imbalance between the classes (Dourlens et al. 1991: 41). However, in all these cases, the limitation that runs through the problematic of risk distribution is that the wish to avoid a series of dangers is taken for granted. In other words, in their ethical explorations, even approaches that treat risk as a cultural product ignore the mechanisms of the differentiated diffusion of threats. Social division does not lie in the unequal distribution of goods and resources, but in the cultural imposition of the fact that it is the social distribution of a specific set of goods and resources in each specific era, that reflects power relations. Risk is no exception to this configuration, although the scale is inverted: possessing resources is here replaced by not being exposed to dangers. It is the socio-cognitive objec- tivation of dangers, or at least of their hierarchy, which, for example, makes unemployment a dreaded probability and not paid leisure time, and makes phobogenic crime a much more unacceptable threat than road accidents. So, one has to ask: is the response to threats through the development of individual precautionary strategies giving rise to an ever-greater concentration of dangers on the classes that have neither the means of prevention nor the possibility of moving away from the sources of dangers? In this case, could the application of individual avoidance strategies be a new central axis around which the social stratification of post-industrial societies is structured? And, if so, how do all these strategies linked to the new control take their place in a highly institutionalized world?

V. THE NEW CONTROL AND THE SOCIETY OF INSTITUTIONS

The emergence of the new control indicates in itself that some remarkable transformations are occurring, reshaping both formal and informal powers and the modes of compliance needed to sustain them. The conventional wisdom that looked for the marks of domination in the mirror of social regulation is obsolete. The relationship between controller and controlled is now valid only for a precise time or space. They have no further interest in each other outside of these limits, within which both seek to reduce their contact to the minimum necessary to extract mutual benefits. In an extraordinary reversal of the situation, they find themselves natural allies against a dangerousness that is more supposed than real, and largely generated by the alliance that it is thought to threaten. The new control naturally produces its own excluded groups. But its functions of traditional regulation, operating through hegemonic values, have disappeared. This development, which is very important in itself, in no way indicates that the control now serves for anything other than the implementation of stratified relationships; on the contrary, it reveals and reflects the silent revolution that these relationships are undergoing in the transition from the level of relations between groups to the level of relations between institutions and individuals, or, increasingly, between institutions. The "institutional individual," whether employee, client or user, is only a spare part, whose interest lies strictly in performing its role. For this purpose, her differences and incompatibilities must be limited to the spaces intended for this use, where she will have every opportunity to play another role that enables her to develop her "difference" far beyond the traditional social limits. So long as her roles are not mixed between institutional machines, no control structure will intervene. The polysemic act, imbued with a culture of personal interaction, gives way to monosemic performance, inspired by the socio-cognition of access to the institution. Forms of control adapted to this development are constantly generated and, in turn, influence the "social" bond in non-social directions. The macroscopic impact of these transformations is enormous. They have already absorbed and are rapidly eliminating the value-based mediation of power relations, an element without which human society hitherto seemed inconceivable. The potential of the society of institutions is immense and goes far beyond that currently envisaged by social theory. A separate analysis must be devoted to this topic alone. For our present purpose, we must briefly recapitulate the major characteristics of the new control in a way that makes it possible to examine its link with the economy of power that generates it and the mechanisms of social homogenization and differentiation that dispense it.

V.1 From the Direct to the Institutional

Let us start by sorting the developments described in the previous chapters according to categories that apply to the development of sociality. Firstly, institutional control does not emerge spontaneously from social relations; it is a *managerial, impersonal* product embedded in the planned mode of organization and interaction of the post-industrial world. Secondly, it is *integrated* in an act or activity, often administrative, as part of its meaning and purpose. This activity is not exclusively or mainly one of control and it is impossible to distinguish between its "controlling" aspects and the others. Thirdly, institutional control is often *beneficial* and sometimes even *liberating*, rather than constraining, since it is a precondition for, or is often part of, a service offered to the population of its domain, i.e. its "users." Fourthly, it thus succeeds in becoming *consensual*, even *collaborative*, since its utility lies in providing processes and protections that give a satisfactory result in defending each against the others. Finally, as a consequence, it is *dangerizing* and therefore, unlike spontaneous control, *atomizing*. It applies centrifugal forces that erode collective bonds and fragment community relationships as it substitutes fear of others for normative prescriptions.

All this represents a great compromise that deeply transforms the economy of power. The close relationship, the group, and the community lose their capacity to generate compliance insofar as their members are now regulated by contexts and environments with which they are obliged to interact and collaborate. It is the qualitative dimensions of this shift from direct social regulation to hetero-regulation that are most important. What is asked of the user of a regulating process is a compliance implying neither loyalty nor interdependence, as would be the case for a structure of direct sociality. The priorities of

action do not establish either promises or guarantees for
the future. The integration of the user into the framework
of his activity is identified with the fulfilment of certain
preliminary conditions, often dependent on another institution. For example, so long as my bank confirms to my
supermarket that it accepts the charge for my purchases,
I am a "normal" customer going through the check-out.
This in no way implies that tomorrow's purchase will go as
smoothly. Indeed, it takes away all meaning from creating
relationships, since no power of decision exists in that
context to provide any grounds for motivation to assess
the future. Unlike the isolated shopkeeper, no supermarket employee can give us a product free of charge
or treat us as a "good customer." This disinvestment of
direct sociality is not merely a symptom of "disaffiliated"
relations or "disembedded" activities, as is often thought.
It is a positive, managed, albeit involuntary, development, engendered by a paradoxical combination of two
competing tendencies: on the one hand, the natural quest
to break free from collective and personalized power, and
on the other hand, for the first time in the history of the
species, a degree of reliability in relations with impersonal
sources going beyond that of relations of close sociality.

It is precisely the balance of this competition that illus-
trates the rapid transition from direct sociality to the society
of institutions. From this standpoint, modernity represents
an intermediate stage where the battle of two rival modes of
sociality force institutions into an artificial strategic compromise in which they must support principles and objectives
alien to their strict interests. The moral orthopaedics that
had to run through the spirit and practices of institutions,
from the civil service to industry, and from school to prison,
was only a temporary grafting of premodern sociality onto
the liberal body of the institutions. At its apogee, the bour-

geoisie was content with the accumulation of institutional powers and the legitimation of its powers by the culture of the old monarchical world. This pact of two socialities and the two classes that embody them concluded with the invention of a proletariat proclaimed morally fit only for industrial work and an "incorrigible" underclass deserving only punishment.[113]

However, capitalism expands the spaces where institutional organization is subject to competition and sets in motion a dynamics of relationships that ever more closely obey the rationality of the industrial workshop: monosemic communities that are increasingly gathered around production and hetero-regulated. In parallel, opportunities increase for an urban life served by large-scale systems of administration and production, allowing the isolation of the nuclear family and centred on employment and consumption. The circle of direct sociality and of its accompanying normativity shrinks. The space abandoned is immediately taken over by the diversification of services offering a new territory to the market and, at the same time, by the fragmentation of norms according to the environment that one enters as a user. Experiences are no longer homogeneous, neither are their limits. The fascist and Nazi movements were precisely founded on the sense of loss of control and the desire to reshape the social around community values that would thus govern all institutions. From the firm to the state and from the research laboratory to the sports club, everything must return to the application of a normativity so artificial in conditions

---

113 On the state strategies and "philanthropic" strategies assigned to this historically indispensable bifurcation, see Garland (1985: 50ff). The importance of the distinction between the "deserving" and the "undeserving" poor is seen clearly in works on the relationship between punishment and the industrial revolution; see, for example, Ignatieff (1980) and Melossi and Pavarini (1981).

of modern institutionalization that it needs to generate its own enemies. The Second World War increased in the West both the permeability of society to the institutions of the private sector and the efforts of public institutions to ensure the social equity required to reduce the attraction of applied socialism. The welfare state replaced the last vestiges of collective interdependence and took away the normative prescriptions of its concrete motivations. The transformation was so radical that it brought to the surface a second layer of socialization, that of women, who, between the employment market and the welfare state, found a margin to defy direct social control and to construct themselves outside of their roles in the family and community structures. The culmination of the competitive process between the socially direct and the institutional is exemplified by the "affluent worker," whose emergence signalled the victory of the liberal and entrepreneurial society of institutions. The affluent worker represents a miniature version of the bourgeois, having the same resources and beliefs but to a lesser degree (Goldthorpe et al. 1969): material possessions, education, hobbies, social recognition, values, etc. He embodies the first generalized appearance of an autonomous individual, capable of maintaining his material, cultural, and personal standing without drawing on the resources of a collectivity. The realization of this historic utopia can be understood as the social equivalent of the invention of the wheel. It precipitates the decline of direct sociality and spontaneous social control. The generations that follow legitimately see themselves as the actors of biographical projects whose limits, in terms of prescriptions as much as resources, are defined by institutions. That is why they direct all the energy of their challenges toward the state and the great industrial interests. The movements of the 1960s and 1970s in Western countries expressed the will not to reduce, but to expand and accelerate the society of institutions so that individuals free themselves as quickly as possible from collective sociality and replace it with minimal constraints. It is clear that, contrary to what one thinks when looking close-up, this project has entirely succeeded. However, it is equally clear that the normalization of this condition leads to unexpected consequences, especially after the collapse of the regimes of applied socialism, which were founded on a rival and closely monitored sociality. The state reduces its level of commitment toward these autonomous, fragmented individuals, handing them over to the competition of private institutions, which, as a consequence, undergo a major and transnational expansion. This obliges individual autonomy to transform itself into a solitary experience and eliminates direct structures of communication and negotiation that could normalize the individual project from its birth. Everything that is conceivable must be possible; television and the Web are there to prove it. Social stratification loses the greater part of its legitimacy and becomes identified with a simple condition of access to the institutions of the market, knowledge, information, protection, etc. Post-industrial citizens are left with no alternative but to see themselves as competitors in a space exclusively determined by institutional activities, which alone can offer them an identity, a meaningful hierarchical position, and the material conditions that accompany it.

The consequence is a faster replacement of social interconnection by formal mediation. This is why the concept of "social exclusion" describes both the fear of some and the actual state of others. Social division shifts to new territories; it integrates the new categories of competition and represents them by new criteria. Intersubjective skills are naturally little valued, except in their superficial dimension of "human-resource management." The signs of extensive involvement in, or access to, formal organizations are, by contrast, sufficient in themselves to construct a socially hierarchized position. Personal status is composed of modules provided from outside, granted contractually to the holder and withdrawn once the terms of the contract are no longer fulfilled. A previously and unilaterally defined threshold governs our credibility and isolates us to admonish and punish by '"disconnecting"' us from the game, which is equivalent to taking from us a part of ourselves. One only needs to overstep one's bank overdraft limit to realize one's identity deficit; one only needs to be fired from one's job to be never again the same person. Such developments are specific to the post-industrial world. Access to institutions regulates social relations through the competition and isolation that it generates. Control and stratification are now aligned, much more than in the past of western societies. This identification carries the unprecedented power of the formal organization of social relations and consolidates the shared awareness of the new means of competition and integration; only the skilful manipulation of these two categories offers a high-class position. It is no longer necessary to possess the industrial machine, but it is necessary to be able to benefit from the functioning of the organizational machines. The victory of institutional sociality over direct sociality can thus be summed up in a remarkable equation: the most successful are the most conformist; for they do not pursue a rival action project – scientific, industrial, military, artistic, or intellectual – but instead rely on existing forces to maximize their influence. Just as a business consortium no longer succeeds by eliminating its rivals but by absorbing them, so the post-industrial citizen must show himself more effective than others in predicting developments and exploiting the rules of the established game. He is a socioeconomic investor who, like financial investors, constructs his portfolio by accumulating advantages useful at the different stages of his ideal trajectory: he pursues an education that opens the door to a powerful institution; he cultivates an engaging and tolerant personality that maximizes the chances of getting others to collaborate as he wishes; he makes prudent commitments in personal and family life from which he has to be able to detach himself quickly, pursues a strategic construction of his profile to attract competing institutions, makes adequate provisions for his retirement, etc. The compartmentalized individuality of this strategic trajectory obviously discounts the usefulness of collective contributions and correspondingly increases the importance of the temporal management of one's resources within a strict time framework. A delay in his educational path or a gap in his CV immediately places the social investor in another category. The present is little more than a function of the future. This explains the radical bifurcation between compliance and deviance, expressed ever more sharply and at ever younger ages. This bifurcation is no longer based on material inequalities (which play their important role after it) but around a projected future, a social "potential" that is already foreseeable, as much for the losers as for the winners. The gap between social aspiration and the probable future becomes ever more visible and easy to calculate, while the social environment has no influence that can compensate for shortfalls in training, socialization or motivation. "Second chances" are again offered through institutions, either as social services, or as state, local, or charitable aid initiatives. No one can any longer look after her neighbour's children when she has to go to work; no one can ask a friend to "put in a word" to get his child taken on as an apprentice because he is "getting into trouble." These roles are reserved for social workers and human resource managers, respectively, who have their own criteria for quality and action. There are no loopholes – no control without integration, no integration without success, no success without competition, and no competition without losers, who (to return to the starting point) will be naturally less controllable.

The problem of the post-industrial citizen, and especially of one who finds himself on the wrong side of normality, is precisely that one cannot just "be." At every moment one has to be someone and somewhere, ahead of or behind others. The problem of control is a corollary of this: why should one espouse the criteria of a future irretrievable delay as one's rules of life? What is the sense of following a calm, efficient, regular order for which one cannot even hope to serve as an alternative or even as an alibi but only as a warning scarecrow? The impact of hope and repression is limited by the precise awareness of individual positioning, for the present and for the future. Only spontaneous and disorganized disorder can provide a brief but gratifying consolation for those who have lost their motivation. Deviance thus constructs itself as a by-product of institutional regularity. This explains why it is perceived as a cancerous development of the social tissue that must simply be stopped without endangering the processes that produce it, as a general social phenomenon rather than as a multitude of unrelated events. Because the fact that we are controlled in itself constitutes a success, the issue of deviance presents itself in terms of efficacy, not princi-ple.[114] We are probably moving toward a formal conceptual separation between the controlled and the uncontrolled, in which the latter constitute another of the post-industrial tribes that the institutions have not entirely succeeded in managing. However, if one takes account of the enor-mous deficit produced by the withdrawal of direct social control, one has to concede that here too the institutional web has won a great victory. Contrary to conservative fears and progressive hopes, no threat of explosion seems to weigh on the macrostructure of institutional capitalism. While the integrated enjoy their satisfying relationship with the organizations, the "excluded', both victims and offenders, suffer together in the hope of greater access to the institutions and deeper integration into the main-stream. Conformism and revolt, configured in formal and symmetrical channels, are indeed bundled together in a single offer. The major socio-technical systems now hold all the keys to the social know-how.

V.2 From Discipline to the Vacuum

The transformation of sociality naturally corresponds to transformations of the mechanisms of production and distribution of power. Social control, being only a concep-tual category linking these mechanisms to the organization of a given society, undergoes the same transformations, requiring us to pose the fundamental question: where is power today? Where should we look for the capacity of insti-tutional sociality to function effectively, to perpetuate and extend itself? The intense institutionalization of the social

---

114 This explains the apparent paradox that post-industrial citizens want both "more severe punishments" for offenders and "other ways of punishing minor offences," as well as the fact that they strongly reject any attempt to address the issue as a private problem (e.g. considering self-defence as a means of response to phobogenic deviance) (Grémy 1998: 147).

world and the permanent growth of the concentration of
power in institutions – at once the symptom and the cause
of a dangerized and perioptic society – have to be seen as
facets of a comprehensive development that interpenetrate
and explain each other. The centrality of the institution is
based on the atomization of the social, which the institution supports, and this atomization, in turn, is based on the
dangerization of the society of institutions. To develop a
contemporary problematic of power, one must assimilate
the institution as a point of convergence of competing
positionings that may be collaborative or stratified. This
centrality contrasts with the atomized position of the individual actor. Simply by virtue of its existence, the institution
already bears a message that addresses – and in doing so
surpasses – several categories of individuals (users, clients,
employees, observers, etc.). It is the necessary and common
priority, the quintessence of this centrality, that configures
this multitude of acts and thoughts, ranging from the wish
to consume to submission to the rules. The almost exclusive
aim, therefore, is to extend this centrality ever further, to
colonize more time, space, and consciousness by increasing
the frequency of the acts and the number of actors. This
formidable force leads to the necessary enlargement of the
content of individual consciousness, which stretches and
changes shape like an elastic bag into which more and more
objects are pushed. The multiplication of the options for
thinking and acting expands monastic internal experience,
which is already organized according to categories of formal
organization. The institution thus becomes an instrument
whose capacity to exercise power is the direct and necessary
consequence of the social "addressability" that forms its
raison d'être. Power is no longer expressed in the decisions
of the powerful, but in the strategic diversified decisions
of the weak. It lies in the modules and interstices of this

strategic framework, in the gaps between the atomized subjects who obtain their own power through access to the institutions. Thus, the more they succeed in their project, the more they contribute to the schema that controls them, since the institution holds a quantum of power for each of its users. Just as the business conglomerate with a reasonable profit margin on a world market is infinitely more powerful than the neighbourhood shop whose margins are much higher, institutions levy their "'commission'" of power on each fragment of action and consciousness. The rate of commission is much lower than that of traditional social collectivities, from the tribe to the extended family, or even modern collectivities, such as the group of friends or the nuclear family; but it extends over vast sets of behaviours, themselves generated by the proliferation of the options available at each instant. Above all, it is made up of fragments that are cumulable and manipulable as concentrations of knowledge, as information and, finally, as new projects of action. Such capital, magnificently exemplified today by computer software that is used worldwide, is made up of nothing other than individual options established on the assumption that they are unavoidable because they have been chosen by the great majority of others. It is sufficient to control the gap between actors in order to control the actors themselves. The stake of in control thus shifts from the imposition of a specific world among several possible worlds to the "'free'" construction of one possible world.

While the position of pre-industrial and post-industrial formations in this transition is relatively clear, modern institutions find themselves in a phase of rapid adaptation. The cultural, organizational, or political sovereignty expressed by the school, the factory, and the state is clearly in crisis, because its object and especially its way of governing are proving to be obsolete. The sovereign institutions, which are supposed to represent and reinforce an imagined collectivity constructed around the nation state, are being overtaken by managerial institutions. These are flexible and ready to be shaped by the objects of their management, and, even more importantly, inclined to displace their own sovereignty toward their users. The eagerness to charm with "decentralization," "consultation," and "openness to society" is, with astonishing speed, transferring the principles of "client-driven management" to areas where formal prescription used to be the self-evident rule. The absolute masters of childhood, the moral pedagogues who made free use of corporal punishment, have become the facilitators of knowledge and citizenship. Foremen and middle managers are mentors who must support, train, and motivate their subordinates in accordance with principles of efficient human-resource management. The structures of political governance, from the neighbourhood council to the new supranational bodies, refrain from judgements and free decisions, and invent discourses and initiatives to counter the "democratic deficit." The school has had to compete with television; the factory and the office with leisure; and the state with the shopping mall. Discipline, an accessory function of industrial, moral, or civic sovereignty is in rapid retreat as a form of control. It cannot deliver a power that is too subtle to present itself as such and too sophisticated to be dispensed homogeneously. Physical and moral "training[115]" is replaced by education in making decisions and managing threats. There is neither a precise goal nor an overall project. To express the new power, control relinquishes sovereign domination and takes the form of a qualitative, regulating dimension of social mediation.

A new type of domination is thus underway. To make it

---

115 Translator's note : « dressage » in the original text, as a reference to a central element of disciplinary control, particularly as conceived by Foucault.

intelligible, we must examine its nuances. The erosion of the collective and the competition between poles of perioptivity indicate the fragmentary organization of this new domination. The regulating processes define it as based on a repetition of skills acquired through the use of sociotechnical systems. The hyper-regular action frameworks reveal it as a determining function of the consciousness of post-industrial experience. The fear of others shapes it as a series of defensive decisions, made on a case-by-case basis. Running through and uniting all its qualities is a "chronobehavioural" dimension, i.e. a learning through consciousness and action whose invisible coherence is brought about differently at each moment, according to the assessment of the circumstances and the modalities of the target task.

The new control is made up of elastic, heterogeneous, temporal units that last the time it takes for them to be perceived as coherent enough to form "a thought" or "an act." The perioptic attraction is expressed in abrupt, intermittent, multiple ways: a road sign, an advertisement, a queue, or a calculation to find a place to park. These moments of mostly unconscious alignment with the organizing schemas that encompass us make up a very high proportion, if not the majority, of our experiences in late modernity. I propose the term *anthropomoment* to designate these thematically different but qualitatively identical modules of compliance. The basis of their unity is their insertion in normality, constructed by limits that do not appear as prescriptive but assert themselves as given, precisely on account of the quantity of anthropomoments that they capture. The self-proliferating dynamics that is set up determines without distinction both the awareness and the norm. The anthropomoment is not a reflection of internalization but the molecule from which the norm is constructed. It is without consequence when no institution captures and regenerates it in its centrality; but it is all-powerful when it is part of a great totality of convergence. It does not follow the rule but creates it and reproduces it. This explains the seemingly paradoxical split between gentle organizational compliance and the substrate of violence that entertains us in a video game, fascinates us on television, and scares us in everyday life. High regularity and the breakdown of the rules coexist without major conflict a few miles apart precisely because the same social molecules may either be coalesced by a structure or exist in a free state. This is never more obvious than in the case of vandalism, an act that often requires more application and discipline than everyday activities like waiting in line or stopping at traffic lights. But the moment a person covers the walls of his neighbourhood with graffiti is not (yet!) integrated into a structure that imposes its rule on the act; however, the opposite is true for the virtual world, where systematic destruction is a worldwide teenage pastime. These anthropomoments, although constructed around a kind of consciousness that is not very different, are captive, organized, and therefore regulated in the broad perioptic arrangement of the institutional web. It is their relationship with a structured activity that makes them controllable and not their content, their collective adherence to a mode of practice and not the thoughts that may be associated with them.

The notion of the anthropomoment makes it possible to understand the volatility of the individual as a fundamental social actor who can no longer be '"compacted"' into reasonably homogeneous groupings. It also permits the osmosis between the internal world, the experiential world, and the social world without requiring us to separate the analysis into insulated stages, an approach that is proving increasingly inadequate when exploring contemporary western society. By producing a transversal perspective that seeks to break down the barriers between partial problematics, the anthropomoment simultaneously represents the socio-cognitive dimension of the post-industrial universe and launches the analysis of domination in this universe. The anthropomoment is the only meaningful unit when contact with institutional power is concerned, and therefore the only unit of socialized communication in the post-industrial world. The structured management of chronobehavioural modules is the everyday face of power.

Thus, we return to the understanding of control and deviance in terms of disruption. As regards its social function, the institution is only a platform for the capture and treatment of anthropomoments and, by the same token, a machine for binary scission between captive and non-captive moments. This process, policed by its own regularity, can be threatened by rebellious moments that penetrate its environment without belonging to it, like grains of sand in the cogs of a machine. They are immediately identified and generally crushed without leaving any traces. But, they can create problems if they exceed a certain threshold and affect the quality of the overall process. That is why life in run-down urban areas is like driving a car in a poor state of repair: when it works, there is a constant fear of breakdown; when it doesn't work, one doesn't drive any longer. In other words, precisely because of the perioptic organization of anthropomoments there are no intermediate forms of sociality. These instants that an institutional process cannot or will not capture are exiled into an abandoned world that does not have visible rules. Minute regulation and the total non-existence of laws can alternate moment by moment in the life of the same person. There only has

to be a sufficiently wide gap between institutional actions
for us to become aware of this. These gaps open up much
more easily for those who are not attractive as users for
private institutions and not powerful enough to get this
lack replaced by the intervention of public institutions, in
a word, for the poor and the immigrants. It is only a matter
of time before the repetitions of this institutional deficit
lead to the production of individuals who integrate it into
their identity. This vicious circle reduces even further the
likelihood of making up the deficit.

The new control produces its own deviants in an original
way: it deprives them of the rules while demanding that they
behave as if the rules were in place. Post-industrial sociality
requires whole communities to align themselves on a mode
of coexistence mediated by institutions, even those who
do not have access to this mediation. The contradiction
is flagrant. How are these attached anthropomoments to
be produced among people who are not capable of being
captured by the institutional web? They have been stripped
of the traditional means of control, such as the imposition of collective values, domination within the family, the
assignment of low social aspirations, etc. These traditional
mechanisms are now culturally ineffective and often legally
forbidden. In parallel, the contemporary means of control
are totally identified with those of social stratification.
Therefore, they are by definition unavailable to those who
find themselves at the bottom of the ladder. It is another
novelty of late modernity that the same mode of control is
applied across the spectrum of classes without regard to the
different resources they may have at their disposal. Unlike
sovereign power, institutional power is egalitarian, but only
in its design, not its availability. So what should surprise us
is not that deviance is increasing, but that there is so little of
it. This is probably the greatest tribute to Gramsci's theses

on cultural hegemony and the construction of a consensus on domination. But, beyond this aspect, it is a development that establishes the structuring of normality outside a culture composed of conscious elements and the consensus that it can produce. The manipulation of social gaps is sufficient to construct a socio-cognition regulating any relationship, even the relationships that, by their nature, contravene this regulation. Deviance can no longer establish itself in its traditional social meaning of another world animated by other desires and subject to other rules. It is only perceived as a deficient activity, a broken sociality, or a low-quality life option. Far from being able to impose its difference as a rival activity, it is determined by its perception and by the fear it arouses. It is quite simply the antithesis of the regularity that institutions sustain, and its existence proves their absolute power. Thus, a bank robber with a revolver is much less frightening than a "tough" teenager with a blade, because the latter moves into and out of normative reality without an action framework, without attachments, without principles and, therefore, without limits. He switches on and off as a socialized subject and a rational actor. Unlike the institutional reality that produces him, he is unpredictable; his anthropomoments are too random, which is sufficient to justify the fear he arouses.

V.3 The Paradox of Security and the Economy of Suspicion

The new control is an extraordinary mechanism of destruction. It wipes out whole species of behaviours from the map of human socio-diversity. This extinction takes place on two parallel axes: the hyper-regular contraction of the limits of permitted behaviours and the suppression of areas of consciousness and action in which doubt and uncertainty can exist as normal conditions. The first is a direct consequence of the propagation of devices for managing behaviours. The second stems from the combination of this management with the institutional capacity to guarantee the content of the perioptic diffusion of their operation. From this standpoint, the institution is merely a machine that makes the world predictable. Banishing doubt is not a project for post-industrial societies but the pre-condition for their central project, which is directed toward the production of intended futures, radically different from the present. In contrast to traditional sociality, which uses doubt strategically to impose beliefs, the society of institutions treats every form of uncertainty as a failure, a weakness of its control structures, which clearly include the structures of knowledge besides those of behavioural normalization. What is unknown is potentially dangerous and, in the diversity of its manifestations, becomes the object of the "precautionary principle." This non-normality of the uncertain casts its shadow on all the fields where institutions can produce intended results. Things as diverse as eating habits, road traffic, pension plans, and sexual relations now converge under the incessant demand for more control and certainty. The "risk society" is in reality a simple and partial reflection of the institutional capacity to secure a high degree of certainty and to legitimately promise an ever wider and deeper certainty. The society of institutions is not mainly a risk society, but a control society that, in its formidable success and its competitive structure, cannot prevent its users from acquiring a significant awareness of the dangers that it promises to eliminate (Lianos 1999). Institutional management of the immense, collective, total dangers leads post-industrial citizens to see the occurrences of such dangers as abnormal events. This structural contradiction, which I call the *paradox of security* (Lianos & Douglas 2000), is the main motivating process in modern societies. It is through this fault line that enters the defensive, probabilistic reasoning of a total, self-sufficient, guaranteed security, covering the whole trajectory of individual and family life. This reasoning elevates hesitation and caution to the level of primordial socioeconomic skills; it is the price to be paid when one decides to avoid what cannot be controlled in advance.

Here lies a fundamental problem: while institutions flourish in their expert competition to produce an ever more manageable, predictable, and transparent reality, individuals find themselves powerless in the face of a rapidly growing deficit in means and skills. More precisely, this deficit is constructed between the experience mediated by institutions and the experience of individuals, families, or groups, i.e. the experiences in which the individual must mobilize her own resources. This second type of experience is increasingly surrounded by circumstances that are not congenial to it and often completely hostile. This implies not just a deskilling of the social subject, but a total reversal of her context of consciousness and life. It is like a car breakdown on the highway; one can only seek institutional support to deal with it, because the environment is entirely configured for that. The individual is a structural element to be handled by competent bodies, such as the breakdown rescue organization, to which one has to be linked in advance. The old world, in which we could wave to a passing driver and ask to be towed to the next garage, is simply inconceivable. The same goes for all dimensions of post-industrial life: it is, for example, impossible to be a good parent without cooperating efficiently with the school or the kindergarten. But, it is also impossible to be a bad parent without the collaboration of the social services. Although her skills and knowledge grow constantly, there are very few matters in which the individual can compete with the institution, because she suddenly finds herself a generalist, however broadly competent, in a world constructed and controlled by specialists, user in a world of producers who take charge of everything, including her own sociality. The deficit of the social subject, whether individual or spontaneously collective, thus deepens as a parameter of her own interests: it is the perioptic attachment to guaranteed institutional functionalities that places the subject in a context configured by her suppliers. This naturally exacerbates the need for foresight and vigilance, since the post-industrial subject, far from being incompetent, juggles exceedingly well all the balls that institutions throw at her. But, the subtler the game becomes, the more it is important not to receive balls with different, or, worse, unknown specifications. Control is rapidly translated into foresight and judgement into suspicion; this in a nutshell is the problem that arises as much for the citizens of late modernity as for the institutions concerned with the relations among them, like the school, the social services, the police or the municipal authority. How can the multitalented, but also suspicious and vulnerable subject be placed in an environment of confidence? How can a reassuring predictability be restored in certain parts of a universe that sets up as a criterion of performance an immediate adaptability to the new conditions that it constantly generates? In other words, how can functions of direct sociality be kept alive in the era of institutions?

Contradictory demands can only be satisfied by the use of superior resources. The first victims of defensive attitudes are found, as we have seen, among the lower classes. There are two reasons for this. On the one hand, the middle and upper classes are able to make the institutional functions work in their favour and get better returns on their predictions, thanks to their greater knowledge of the institutional dynamics. On the other hand, these classes can completely cut off their social contact with the lower classes, precisely because of their extreme precaution and thanks to the institutional mediation that distances the worker from the living environment of the user. It goes without saying that for the rest of the "active population" this distancing is even greater. This social economy, made up of suspicion, and the ensuing flight to which it leads, represents the stratifying dimension of institutionality. Social division is not constructed and legitimated by the direct exercise of power between classes, since all classes suffer from a growing deficit in the face of the institutions. It is built on the capacity to manage the security paradox more or less effectively and to live in an environment that enables one to achieve this efficacy. Control, thus, emerges naturally as the central axis of social division, since a condition or person that can be construed as less reliable, as unpredictable, or even uncontrollable not only bears a mark of dangerousness, but also, and more profoundly, represents par excellence the lower-quality option. After the accumulation of material possessions, financial resources, and scientific knowledge, we now accumulate a capital of certainty and security.

Social control, exerted as an activity imposing direct limits on social behaviours, becomes an impossible task in late modernity. That is why post-industrial police forces are unable to bridge the gap between brutal violence and impotence. They have been assigned a role of agency of last resort for which they have not been prepared; in contrast to the integrated services available to the users of institutions that operate in a context of compliance, there is no "one-stop shop" for deviants. This reflects a simple fact: when perioptic motivation fails to transform the individual into

a hyper-regular, self-sufficient, self-limited social unit, there
is no other means left to integrate him; in accordance with
the rules of probabilistic reasoning, he will be treated with
suspicion and therefore immediate isolation. Direct social
control is a victim of the unprecedented flexibility of the
institutional web that provides individuals with the resources
to circumvent the dysfunctions of their social life at a lower
cost than that of dealing with them. Law is supplanted by
suspicion and the competition not to be subject to it. This
new social division clearly benefits women and old people
and places men under the test of security screening. One
little false note in the hyper-regular melody, a slightly
abrupt movement, a beard, a more intense expression,
worn-out clothes, or a baseball cap is enough to activate the
daily sorting of strangers and help construct our security
reflexes. These automatic reactions, both arbitrary and
rigid, quickly lead to stratified conceptual groupings. Social
control works more on hypothesis than on reality and limits
itself to an epidermic relation to others, governed by fear
and avoidance. This state of affairs, specific to the society of
institutions, strongly polarizes the functions of social regulation, which are concentrated on the one hand around
the "good pupils," whose learning of regularity is sufficient
for them to lead their lives without the need for formal
external interventions, and the "bad pupils," who quickly
exhaust the capacities of these interventions. Both are in
deficit in relation to the institutions that constantly try to
train them in ever subtler and deeper ways. But, while the
former benefit from their deficit, the latter suffer from it.
To reduce this disparity would require new motivating structures capable of re-attaching those who detach themselves
from the regular pathways to some fundamental aspects of
the perioptic universe. Formal repression and monitoring
cannot function effectively in a context where regulation

is a parameter of individual consciousness and not of collective practice. This failure often masks the extent of an unprecedented success. The society of institutions has rapidly succeeded in establishing a model of social relations to replace the value-based regulation of direct sociality that it killed off. This "great regularization," which has taken place in the last 30 years, completely redefines control as a function of individual, external compliance, compatible with all beliefs, and all moralities – even if they oppose each other – and also with their absence! Never have we been further from witch-hunts and totalitarian utopias, at least since the Athenian agora. This masterpiece of bourgeois citizenship is indeed to be admired, not because we could not have done better, but because it has been imposed as the best that we could have done. Nonetheless, one needs to point out the dynamics of the tendencies implied in this transition and the transforming potential that this new model of control contains.

V.4 Periopticism and Participation: "Social" Control?

I have outlined a context that makes it possible to conceive "institutional control'" as a factor embedded in the development of the institution, even as a constituent factor of all institutionality, including relations at the level of individual options (consumption, circulation, planning, etc.). This transition implies the idea that *the major part of what can be called control does not relate either to practices of constraint or to activities oppressing behaviour and expression, but to the organization and contextualization of what is often optional, or even desired by a sovereign subject.* What belongs to the sphere of control depends neither on the consciousness of the subject or group involved nor on the will of the actor who produces the effect in question, but on the conditions created by their interaction. This does not mean that control is "neutral" in terms of either production or reception, but it does suggest that there is no reason to assume a direct correspondence between these two stages. It is, therefore, necessary to recognize the existence of frameworks of activity where control arises in several ways that were often not designed to produce such an effect. I have argued in the previous chapters that no will to promote and constitute a coherent cognitive and moral world in the user can be imputed to the institution. The only objective the institution pursues is to obtain behaviours conducive to its functioning, i.e. to its expansion. The focus of concern for institutional control can therefore no longer be seen as an extension of subjection, either in the sense of a submission or in its Foucauldian sense of the constitution of the socialized human being as a subject. The comprehensive modernist vision of control no longer functions in the great majority of contemporary interactions, which are by definition socio-technical. On the contrary, we are seeing a '"de-subjection"' of the individual, produced by a fragmented accentuation in her dimension as a multiple user, since the aim of control is to regulate exclusively the praxic activity linked to the institution and not other acts, thoughts, or emotions. But, even if the final objective of a perioptic disposition is not surveillance, it should not be ruled out that it forms *de facto* a new model of control. As a structure, it clashes with the nature of social communication and consequently with the constitutive processes of culture and sociality. In the context of consumption, this signals the colonization of the temporal, cognitive, and even spatial horizons – which previously belonged to the practices of social referentiality– by private, bipolar considerations exclusively linked to the atomized use of services and goods. The actor is by definition an atomized actor who, through her own probabilistic reasoning, constructs the partitions that separate her from other potential consumers. The monosemy of her gaze is only the reflection of the immense machinery of motivation to which she is subjected. Thus, through the multiplication of this schema, an *involuntary control* is established, organized on the one hand around the service offered, and on the other hand around the cellular privacy of the subject-user. Through its quantitative importance, involuntary control imposes itself as the main structure of social regulation. It can better be conceived as an inherent dimension of any relationship that is not oriented toward the exercise or projection of a model of behavioural compliance, but which brings with it aspects of control by its own nature, through the organization of the elements and interactions that construct it. Involuntary control emerges as a secondary effect of the relationship to which it owes its existence. We have seen that it develops at the expense of the density of direct sociality and the mechanisms that promote it, mainly because of the isolation that the perioptic structure imposes on each observer. However, involuntary control not only addresses precise specific subjects, but also, because its emergence is neither preconceived nor strictly speaking desired, it would be difficult to associate it with the conveying of dominant interests. Hence, one is obliged to follow the precise development that has produced it in order to identify its role. In the context of consumption, one would probably find the following chain: advertising message > sense of relative vulnerability > internalization of probabilistic reasoning > atomization > periopticon > involuntary control.

The only reference of this chain outside the actor is the offered service itself. Nevertheless, it would be inaccurate to say that the blinkers imposed on the actor exist *because of* this service. Rather, their *raison d'être* is rooted in the very process of linking the developments involved,

186 | THE NEW SOCIAL CONTROL: THE INSTITUTIONAL

and these developments in turn exist *in relation to* their common focus, because it is the considerations around this focus that gather a multitude of atomized gazes and not the reverse.

This '"neutral"' disposition, emerging from below, requires new categories of thought in order to be conceptualized in an organized way. One first has to accept the idea of a control leading to a destructuring, an acute desocialization. One also has to dissociate domination from intentional, planned action. Finally, one has to accept the idea of a power residing in the intersection between individuals and institutions, which everyone can use according to the extent of their access to this interstitial space and according to the duration of this access. I shall try to sketch here the relationship between the new control and this power that is produced as a parameter of access to institutions. In the first place it is a functional pact that corresponds to the hegemony of the social independence and institutional dependence of the subject. The new role of control is to represent the advantages of a consensual political and economic management of social coexistence, rather than to suppress attempts at overthrowing the existing stratifying order. The explanation is simple: in the post-industrial society a social movement can neither reverse the hegemony of the others nor establish its own hegemony without the mediation of institutions. The institutional web has become so dense and effective that social conflicts can no longer organize themselves *against* the institutions and their functions but only *about* the fruits of these functions. It is a development that recognizes the undeniable fact that the penetration of social life by public and private goods and services has been able to establish itself as a fundamental element of the experience of the lower classes too. Conflict abandons its traditional focus, i.e. the setting-up of an institutional machine almost exclusively beneficial to the bourgeois. The class struggle in modernity is irreversibly won by the integration of the lower classes into the society of institutions which still bear the signs of their bourgeois origins. It is therefore natural to dispute the legitimacy and the distribution of the profits of this victory that we share universally but inequitably. In parallel, the institutions now make themselves available at the individual level, which provides still inequitable but real opportunities. They enable the isolated subject to construct her own projects of social differentiation and, exceptionally, to successfully complete them. The growing sense of belonging to a vast mass of "middle classes" reflects the fact that everyone seeks to activate institutional functions that are more or less available on an impersonal but stratifying basis. The concentration on the same means of competition also determines the objectives of the process. Power is, therefore, constructed, on these two levels of convergence, which redefine its meaning and its terrain. Perioptic power no longer refers to control but to membership, and no longer applies to persons but to the gaps between them. The control that conducts this power can no longer express itself in norms, because the context of its application is too fluid for persistent models of behaviour to be valorized. On the contrary, what holds together its thematic and temporal fragments, its scattered anthropomoments of contemporary control, is their compatibility with this general process of integration of the directly social in the institutional. The new control is characterized above all by the fact that it breaks with its traditional function of submission and organizes itself around compatibility. It, thus, places itself outside social relations, in the parameters of the configuration of these relations at a higher level of concentration that is

completely opaque for the social subject. This densification produces its own qualitative order and is not a mere
residual effect of the retreat of direct social control. Perioptic control is an effect of the efficient organization that
the society of institutions imposes on its subjects. Thus, it
is not control that is being desocialized but sociality that is
being institutionalized; it is not surveillance that is being
deepened and expanded but the demand for systems and
networks favouring atomized fluidity that is propagating
itself. It is not freedom that is regressing, but its content
that is being displaced. It is not stratification that is disappearing, but its dependence on institutional junctures
that is increasing. It is not the norm and its socializing
functionality that are collapsing, but their foundation that
is being laid away from internalized values.

To what extent can one speak of "social" control in
these conditions of an organizational densification that
externalizes the regulation of post-industrial life? Paradoxically, we are somewhat short of alternative concepts,
mainly because we always regard control as an appendix
of domination, the only interest of which lies in this
relation of dependence, and which can only be usefully
approached in terms of a commitment to a broader
critique.[116] At the other extreme we find an undifferenti-
ated and inert conception of a "social control" that every
society inevitably exercises. I suspect it is the gap between
these two poles that led Stan Cohen (1985: 2) to remark
that social control "has lately become something of a
Mickey Mouse concept." As regards the society of insti-

---

116 Abercrombie, Hill and Turner (1980) have criticized the unqualified
   attribution of the passivity of the subordinate classes to their integration
   into the ideology of the dominant classes; too much emphasis on this
   type of explanation discounts, at the empirical level, the emergence of
   autonomous cultures, and at the theoretical level it represents a misinter-
   pretation of Marxian theory. For another critique, see Giddens (1991).

tutions, this problem is now being resolved through a restructuring so fundamental that it invites a new context of analysis and interpretation. The desocialized character of control is part of a formidable development of institutionality as a coordination and communication function of post-industrial society. The new control is a social control only in its dimension of parallel and identical delivery of the parameters, limits, and constraints that ineluctably determine both the form and the content of human relations. But, it is not at all a *social* control in its structural origin, in its efficient monosemy, or the absence of a will to dominate. If one takes account of the diversity of its forms and the fragmentation of the compliance that it produces, one should rather speak of the particular aspect that is referred to in each case: perioptic, hyper-regular, dangerizing, institutional, or social. This aspect will express only one facet of the new reality of the social subject, who finds himself paradoxically sovereign in the constitution of his identity, his biography, and his social relations, all of which are constructed by modules of institutional mediation.

Desocialized control is neither pure nor static. It coexists in parallel with socially direct or intermediate forms of regulation that correspond to structures of power and domination governed in varying degrees, depending on their historical origins, by different ways of organizing the relations of the social units that take part in them. For example, the ultimate recourse to legitimated violence or to practices of "discipline," as Weber and Foucault described them, is always active in the perioptic organization. "Heavy" policing and the "training" of citizens in primary school persist as forms of control, as do forms of control by interpersonal violence, such as domestic violence, or by a quasi-tribal sociality, such as that of deviant urban gangs or totalitarian sects. But, these

forms are neither dominant nor specific to late modernity, whose main function is precisely to supersede them.
They are often forced to marginalize themselves, either
through secrecy or through a radical opposition to forms
of institutional control; or they are forced to integrate
themselves by espousing its major principles. In any case,
they are now receding from the centre of the social stage,
both as practices and as socio-cognitive categories. It is
always possible that a restructuring of social organization,
especially following a major breakdown of contemporary institutionality (for example, a worldwide financial
crisis) could re-establish them. But it is much more likely
that the degree of this institutionality will raise and that
social relations will become increasingly mediated and
hetero-referential. The interpretative conundrum of
late modernity consists precisely in understanding this
tendency as a dynamics that overdetermines the social
constitution of post-industrial subjects and especially of
their practices, fears, and aspirations. The current shift
to a qualitatively different sociality will crystallize through
the proliferation of vast regulating structures that will
span the planet in real time; it is not certain that such a
regularity will eliminate the diversity of social relations at
all levels, but it seems quite likely. What is more or less
certain is that, in the medium term, world-wide regularization will lead to an entirely vertical control, functioning
through segments of involvement with institutions, and
to the complete marginalization of the "horizontal" social
control that followed the individual through her different
activities and social contacts. Such a development will
finally achieve the goal to which the creation of institutions was aimed: to liberate each of us from the fearful,
inequitable, and often arbitrary constraints that our relations of co-existence impose. But, it will also bring to a

close the period of human history in which collective interdependence and negotiation directly and constantly recreated the social bond instead of submitting to the planning of formal structures of organisation. Those who fear such a future because they consider it less creative should remember that nothing prevents creativity from influencing large-scale social designs. In reality, the danger lies elsewhere – in the total fusion of freedom, satisfaction, and control and in the voluntary passivity that may follow from it. That could reduce our capacity to question the great formative priorities of our societies and lead us to concern ourselves exclusively with the small, the immediate, and the individual. It is likely that in the society of institutions we shall have the power and resources to easily realize the great visions handed down by our history; but it is even more likely that we shall no longer have the will to do so.

Bibliography

Abercrombie, N., S. Hill, and B. S. Turner. *The Dominant Ideology Thesis*. London: Allen & Unwin, 1980.

Abrams, D, and R. Brown. "Self-Consciousness and Social Identity: Self-Regulation as a Group Member." 52, no. 4 (1989): 311-8.

Ackermann, W., R. Dulong, and H. - P. Jeudy. *Imaginaires de l'insécurité*. Paris: Librairie des Méridiens, 1983.

Angell, I. O. "The Place of Information Technology in Global Change." In *Transition to a Global Society*, edited by S. Bushrui, I. Ayman and E. Laszlo. Oxford: Oneworld, 1993.

Archer, D., and L. Erlich-Erfer. "Fear and Loading: Archival Traces of the Response to Extraordinary Violence", Social Psychology Quarterly, Vol. 54, N° 4, 1991." *Social Psychology Quarterly* 54, no. 4 (1991): 343-52.

Augé, M. *Non-Places: Introduction to an Anthropology of Supermodernity*. London: Verso, 1995.

Barr, R., and K. Pease. "Crime Placement, Displacement and Deflection." In *Crime and Justice: A Review of Research*, edited by M. Tonry and N. Morris, 277-318. Chicago: University of Chicago Press, 1990.

Beck, U. *Ecological Politics in an Age of Risk*. Cambridge: Polity Press, 1995.

Bennett, T. "Factors Related to Participation in Neighbourhood Watch Schemes." *British Journal of Criminology* 29, no. 3 (1989): 207-18.

Berger, P., B. Berger, and H. Kellner. *The Homeless Mind*. Harmondsworth: Penguin, 1974.

Bottoms, A. E. "Neglected Features of Contemporary Penal Systems." In *The Power to Punish: Contemporary Penality and Social Analysis*, edited by D: Young, P. Garland. London: Heinemann, 1983.

Bottoms, A. E. "Neglected Features of Contemporary Penal Systems." In *The Power to Punish: Contemporary Penality and Social Analysis*, edited by D. Garland and P. Young. Heinemann, 1983.

Box, S. *Power, Crime and Mystification*. London: Tavistock, 1983.

Box, S., C. Hale, and G. Andrews. "Explaining Fear of Crime." *British Journal of Criminology* 28, no. 3 (1988): 344-9.

Braithwaite, J., and B, Fisse. "Self-Regulation and the Control of

Corporate Crime." In *Private Policing*, edited by C. D. Shearing and P. C. Stenning, 221-246. Newbury Park, California: Sage Publications, 1987.

Capdevielle, J., H. Y. Meynaud, and R. Mouriaux. *Petits boulots et grand marché européen: le travail démobilisé*. Paris: Presses de la Fondation Nationale des Sciences Politiques, 1990.

Carriere, K. D., and R. V. Ericson. *K. D. Carriere and R. V. Ericson, CrimeStoppers: A Study in the Organization of Community Policing*. Toronto: University of Toronto Press, 1989.

Castel, R. *La Gestion des risques*. Paris: Minuit, 1991.

Certeau, M. de. *The Practice of Everyday Life*. Berkeley: University of Cailfornia Press, 1984.

Champion, D. *Measuring Offender Risk: A Criminal Justice Sourcebook*. London: Greenwood Press, 1994.

Clarke, R. V. G. (ed.). *Situational Crime Prevention*. New York: Harrow and Heston, 1992.

Clemente, F., and M. Kleiman. "Fear of Crime Among the Aged." *Gerontologist* 16, no. 3 (1976): 207-10.

Cohen. "Social Control Talk: Telling Stories About Correctional Change." In *The Power to Punish: Contemporary Penality and Social Analysis*, edited by P. Garland and D. Young, 101-29. London: Heinemann, 1983.

Cohen, S. "Introduction." In *Images of Deviance*, edited by S. Cohen. Harmondsworth: Penguin Books, 1971.

Cohen, S. "The Critical Discourse on Social Control': Notes on the Concept as a Hammer." *International Journal of the Sociology of Law*, 1989: 347-57.

—. *Visions of Social Control*. Cambridge: Polity Press, 1985.

Covington, J., and R. B. Taylor. "Fear of crime in urban residential neighborhoods: Implications of between- and within-neighborhood sources for current models." *Sociological Quarterly* 32 (1991): 231-49.

Cumberbatch, G. "The Incidence and Nature of Violence in Television." In *Violence and the Media: Papers presented to a seminiar held by the BBC on 2nd December 1987*. BBC, 1988.

Douglas, M. *Cultural Bias (Occasional Paper no. 34)*. London: Royal Anthropological Institute of Great Britain and Northern Ireland, 1978.

—. *Risk Acceptability according to the Social Sciences*. London: Routledge & Kegan Paul, 1986.

Dourlens C., et al. *Conquête de la Sécurité: Gestion des risques*. Paris: L'Harmattan, 1991.

Ehrenreich, B. *Fear of Falling: The Inner Life of the Middle Class.* New York: Pantheon Books, 1989.

Ekeland, I. *The Broken Dice, and Other Mathematical Tales of Chance.* Chicago: University of Chicago Press, 1993.

Elias, N. *The Civilizing Process: Sociogenetic and Psychogenetic Investigations.* Revised edition. Oxford: Blackwell, 2000.

Erickson, R. V. "Mass Media, Crime, Law and Justice: An Institutional Approach." *British Journal of Criminology* 31, no. 3 (1991): 219-49.

Farrington, D. P. "Predicting Self Reported and Official Delinquency." In *Prediction in Criminology,* edited by Farrington D.P and R. Tarling, 150-71. New York: State University of New York Press, 1985.

Farrington, D. P., and R. (eds.), Tarling. *Prediction in Criminology, State University of New York Press, N. Y., 1985.* New York: State University of New York Press, 1985.

Fattah, E. A. "Les enquêtes de victimisation: leur contribution et leurs limites." *Déviance et Société* 5, no. 4 (1981): 423-40.

Fay, S. J. "The Rise and Fall of Tagging as a Criminal Justice Measure in Britain." *International Journal of the Sociology of Law* 21, no. 4 (1993): 301-17.

Feeley, M., and M. Simon. "Actuarial Justice: The Emerging New Criminal Law ." In *The Futures of Criminology,* edited by D. Nelken, 173-201. 1994.

Feldman, P. *The Psychology of Crime.* Cambridge: Cambridge University Press, 1993.

Ferraro, K. F. *Fear of Crime: Interpreting Victimization Risk.* New York: State University of New York Press, 1995.

Foucault, M. *Discipline and Punish: the Birth of the Prison.* London: Allen Lane, 1975.

France, A. *Le Lys rouge, in Oeuvres.* Paris: Gallimard, 1987.

Fréchet, G. "Technologies de l'information et atomisation du social." *Revue Internationale de l'Action Communautaire* 29, no. 69 (1993): 61-8.

Freitag, M. *Dialectique et société, Vol 2. Culture, pouvoir, contrôle – Les modes de reproduction formels de la société.* Montreal: L'Age d'Homme – Saint Martin, 1986.

Garland, D. "Criminological Knowledge and its Relation to Power: Foucault's Genealogy and Criminology Today." *British Journal of Criminology,* 1992.

—. "Frameworks of Inquiry in the Sociology of Punishment." *British Journal of Sociology,* March 1990: 47.

—. *Punishment and Welfare: A History of Penal Strategies.* Aldershot
(UK): Gower, 1985.

Garland, D., and P. Young. *The Power to Punish: Contemporary Penality
and Social Analysis.* London: Heinemann, 1983.

Garofolo, J. "The Fear of Crime: Causes and Consequences." *Jornal of
Criminal Law and Criminology* 72, no. 2 (1981): 839-57.

Gellner, E. *Culture, Identity and Politics.* Cambridge: Cambridge
University Press, 1987.

Giddens, A. "Four Theses on Ideology." *Revue Canadienne de Théorie
Politique et Sociale* 15, no. 1-3 (1991).

—. *Modernity and Self-Identity: Self and Society in the Late Modern Age* .
Cambridge: Polity Press, 1991.

—. *The Consequences of Modernity.* Cambridge: Polity Press, 1990.

Gillett, G. "Social Causation and Cognitive Neuroscience." *Journal for
the Theory of Social Behaviour* 23, no. 1 (1993): 27-45.

Glaster, D. S. *Bad Guys and Good Guys: Moral Polarization and Crime.*
Westport: Greenwood Press, 1992.

Goffman, E. *Relations in Public: Microstudies of the Public Order.*
London: Allen Lane, 1971.

—. *The Presentation of Self in Everyday Life.* Revised and expanded edn.
London: Allen Lane, 1969.

Goldthorpe, J. H., D. Lockwood, F. Bechhoffer, and J. Platt. *The
Affluent Worker in the Class Structure.* Cambridge: Cambridge
University Press, 1969.

Gras, A. *Grandeur et dépendance: sociologie des macrosystèmes techniques.*
Paris: PUF, 1993.

Grémy, J.-P. "Insécurité et Délinquance." *Actes du colloque 'Risque et société'.*
Cité des sciences et de l'industrie de Paris-La Villette, 1998.

—. *Mesurer la délinquance à partir du témoignage des victimes: l'enquête
pilote IHESI-INSEE de janvier 1999.* Paris: IHESI, 2000.

Gross, J. L., and S. Rayner. *Measuring Culture: A Paradigm for the
Analysis of Social Organization.* New York: Columbia University
Press, 1985.

Gullestad, M. *The Art of Social Relations: Essays on Culture: Social Action and
Everyday Life in Modern Norway.* Oslo: Scandinavian University Press, 1992.

Gunter, B. *Television and Fear of Crime.* London: John Libey, 1987.

Habermas, J. *Legitimation Crisis.* London: Heinemann, 1976.

Habermas, J. "Technology and Science as 'Ideology'." In *Toward a
Rational Society: Student Protest, Science, and Politics.* Boston: Beacon
Press, 1970.

——. *Theory of Communicative Action.* Vol. I. Cambridge: Polity Press, 1991.

Henig, J., and M. G. Maxfield. "Reducing Fear of Crime: Strategies for Intervention." *Victimology* 3 (1978): 297-313.

Hope, T. "Support for Neighbourhood Watch: A British Crime Survey Analysis, HMSO, London." In *Communities and Crime Reduction*, edited by T. Hope and M. Shaw. London: HMSO, 1988.

Hough, M. *Anxiety about Crime: Findings from the 1994 British Crime Survey.* London: HMSO, 1995.

Hough, M., and P. Mayhew. *Taking Account of Crime: Key Findings from the Second British Crime Survey.* London: HMSO, 1985.

Hulsman, L. H. C. "Critical Criminology and the Concept of Crime." In *Abolitionism: Towards a Non-Repressive Approach to Crime*, edited by H. Bianchi and R. van Swaaningen. Amsterdam: Free University Press, 1985.

Ignatieff, M. *A Just Measure of Pain; The Penitentiary in the Industrial Revolution 1750-1850.* London: Macmillan, 1980.

INSEE. *Annuaire statistique de la France.* Paris: INSEE, 1993.

Jacobs, J. B. *Stateville: The Penitentiary in the Mass Society.* Chicago: University of Chicago Press, 1978.

Jeudy, H.-P. *La Peur et les média.* PUF, 1979.

Jones, T., T. Newburn, and D. J. Smith. *Democracy and Policing.* London: Policy Studies Institute, 1994.

Jowell, R., L. Brook, B. Taylor, and G. Prior. *British Social Attitudes: The 8th Report.* Aldershot: Dartmouth, 1991.

Kakalik, J. S., and S. Wildhorn. *The Private Police: Security and Danger.* New York: Crane Russak, 1977.

Katz, S J., and P. (eds) Vesin. *Children and the Media Proceedings of the First International Conference Held in Los Angeles.* Los Angeles: Children's Institute International, 1986.

Kegels, M.-L. "Le crime puisqu'il faut l'appeler par son nom... La peur du crime." *Déviance et Société* 6, no. 2 (1982): 209-20.

Kinsey, R., and S. Anderson. *Crime and the Quality of Life: Public Perceptions and Experiences of Crime in Scotland — Findings from the 1988 British Crime Survey.* Edinburgh: Scottish Office, 1992.

Lagrange, H. et al. *Enquête sur les risques urbains: étude de préfiguration.* Paris: CESDIP, 2000.

Lagrange, H. "La peur à la recherche du crime." *Déviance et société* 17, no. 4 (1993).

Lagrange, H., and S. Roché. *Baby alone in Babylone; deux perspectives d'analyse du sentiment d'insécurité: systèmes d'attitudes et formes de sociabilité en milieu urbain.* Saint Martin d'Hères: CERAT, 1987-89.

Larochelle, G. "Mythe de la révolution technologique et désenchantement postmoderne." *Revue suisse de sociologie* 17, no. 2 (1991).

Lave, J. *Cognition in Practice: Mind, Mathematics and Culture in Everyday Life.* Cambridge: Cambridge University Press, 1988.

Lavrakas, P. J., and E. J. Hertz. "Citizen Participation in Neighborhood Crime Prevention." *Criminology* 20, no. 3-4 (1982): 479-98.

Leeds-Hurwitz, W. *Communication in Everyday Life: A Social Interpretation.* Norwood, New Jersey: Ablex Publishing Corp., 1989.

Legendre, P. *Leçons II – L'empire de la vérité: introduction aux espaces dogmatic industriels, Fayard, 1983, p. 17.* Paris: Fayard, 1983.

Lianos, M. "Point de vue sur l'acceptabilité sociale du discours du risque." *Les cahiers de la sécurité intérieure,* no. 38 - Risque et démocratie. Savoirs, pouvoirs, participation: vers un nouvel arbitrage? (1999): 55-73.

Lianos, M. with Douglas, M. "Dangerization and the End of Deviance." *British Journal of Criminology* 20, no. 2 (special issue on "Criminology and Social Theory") (2000).

Liska, A.E., and W. Baccaglini. "Feeling Safe by Comparison: Crime in the Newspapers." *Social Problems* 37, no. 3 (1990): 361-74.

Loveday, B. "Government strategies for community crime prevention in England and Wales: a study in failure?" *International Journal of Sociology of Law* 22 (1994).

Mair, G., and C. Nee. *Electronic Monitoring: The Trials and their Results.* London: HMSO, 1990.

Mannheim, K. "The Crisis in Valuation." In *Diagnosis of Our Time: Wartime Essays of a Sociologist.* London: Routledge, 1943.

Marx, G. T. "La société de sécurité maximale." *Déviance et société* 12, no. 2 (1988).

Mathiesen, T. "The Future of Control Systems: The Case of Norway." In *The Power to Punish: Contemporary Penality and Social Analysis,* edited by D Garland and P. Young. London: Heinemann, 1983.

Mayhew, P. "Measuring the Effects of Crime in Victimization Surveys." In *Fear of Crime and Criminal Victimization,* edited by W Bilsky, C. Pfeiffer and P. Wetzel. Stuttgart: Ferdinand Elke Verlag, 1993.

Mayhew, P., D. Elliott, and L. Dowds. *The 1988 British Crime Survey.* London: HMSO, 1989.

Melossi, D., and M. Pavarini. *The Prison and the Factory: Origins of the Penitentiary System.* London: Macmillan, 1981.

Miles, I. *Home Informatics: Information Technology and the Transformation of Everyday Life.* London: Pinter Publishers, 1988.

Monjardet, D. "Le modèle français de police." *Les Cahiers de la Sécurité Intérieure* (IHESI), no. 13 (1993): 61-82.

MORI (Market and Opinion Research International). "Public Attitudes to Crime." January 1994.

Nash, M. *Police, Probation and Protecting the Public.* London: Blackstone, 1999.

Nenquin, A. *Discours et pratiques de l'insécurité: la peur de la violence sociale.* Doctoral thesis, Université Paris VII Denis Diderot, 1993.

Nisbet, R. "The Impact of Technology on Ethical Decision-Making." In *The Technological Threat*, edited by J. D. Douglas. Englewood Cliffs, New Jersey: Prentice Hall, 1971.

Ocqueteau, F. "Etat, compagnies d'assurances et marché de la protection des biens." *Déviance et Société* 19, no. 2 (1995).

——. *Gardiennage, surveillance et sécurité privée: commerce de la peur et/ou peur du commerce?* Paris: CESDIP, 1992.

Ocqueteau, F. "How Private Security Sector is Winning its Legitimacy in France." *Interdisziplinäre Studien zu Recht und Staat* 3 (1995).

——. *Les Défis de la sécurité privée: protection et surveillance dans la France d'aujourd'hui.* Paris: L'Harmattan, 1997.

Ocqueteau, F. "L'Etat face au commerce de la sécurité." *L'Année Sociologique* 40 (1990): 97-124.

Ocqueteau, F., and C. Perez-Diaz. *Justice pénale, délinquances, déviances: évolution des représentations dans la société française.* Paris, 1989.

Ocqueteau, F., and M.L. Pottier. *Vigilance et sécurité dans les grandes surfaces.* Paris: L'Harmattan, 1995.

Orwell, G. *Nineteen Eighty-Four.* London: Secker and Warburg, 1949.

Parker, K. D. "Black-White differences in perceptions of fear of crime." *Journal of Social Psychology* 128, no. 4 (1988): 487–94.

Patrie, B, and A. Vogelweith. *La mort hors la loi d'Erick Schmitt : la prise d'otages de la maternelle de Neuilly.* Paris: Austral, 1994.

Pearson, F. S., and J. Toby. "Fear of School-Related Predatory Crime." *Sociology and Social Research* 75, no. 3 (1991): 117-25.

Reiss, A. J. Jr. "Crime Prevention in Urban Communities: A Western Perspective." *Annales Internationales de Criminologie* 30, no. 1-2 (1992).

Riley, D., and P. Mayhew. *Crime Prevention Publicity: An Assessment.* London: HMSO, 1980.

Robert, P. "Insécurité, opinion publique et politique criminelle." *Année Sociologique* 35 (July 1985): 199-231.

Robert, P., and R. Zauberman. "Les victimes entre la délinquance et l'Etat." *Revue de l'Institut de Sociologie,* no. 1-2 (1985): 9-45.

Roché, S. *Le Sentiment d'insécurité.* Paris: PUF, 1993.

Rogers, C. R., and B. F. Skinner. "Some Issues Concerning the Control of Human Behavior." *Science* 124, no. 3231 (November 1956): 1057-65.

Schlesinger, P., and H. Tumber. "Fighting the War against Crime: Television, Police and Audience." *British Journal of Criminology* 33, no. 1 (January 1993).

Schlesinger, P., H. Tumber, and G. Murdock. "The Media Politics of Crime and Criminal Justice." *British Journal of Sociology 42(3):* 42, no. 3 (1991): 397-420.

Schneider, H. J. "Crime in the Mass Media." *Annales Internationales de Criminologie* 30, no. 12 (1992).

Sennett, R., and J. Cobb. *The Hidden Injuries of Class.* Cambridge: Cambridge Universtiy Press, 1972.

Shearing, C., and P. Stenning. "From the Panoptican to Disneyworld: the Development of Discipline." In *Perspectives in Criminal Law.* Aurora, Ontario, 1985.

Shields, R. *Places on the Margin: Alternative Geographies of Modernity.* London: Routledge, 1991.

Shotter, J. *Cultural Politics of Everyday Life: Social Constructionism, Rhetoric, and Knowing of the Third Kind.* Milton Keynes: Open University Press; and University of Toronto Press, 1993.

Simmel, G. *The Philosophy of Money.* 3rd edn. Edited by D. Frisby. Translated by D. Frisby and T. Bottomore. London: Routledge, 2004.

Simon, J. *Poor Discipline: Parole and the Social Control of the Underclass 1890-1990.* Chicago: University of Chicago Press, 1993.

Skogan, W. G. "Communities, Crime, and Neighborhood Organization." *Crime & Delinquency* 35 (1982): 437-57.

Skogan, W. G. "The Fear of Crime and its Behavioural Implications." In *From Crime Policy to Victim Policy,* edited by E. A. Fattah. London: Macmillan, 1986.

Smith, D. J. *Police and People in London: (I) A Survey of Londoners.* London: Policy Studies Institute, 1983.

Smith, L. *Concerns about Rape.* London: HMSO, 1989.

Spierenburg, P. *The Spectacle of Suffering.* Cambridge: Cambridge University Press, 1984.

Steinbruner, J.D. *The Cybernetic Theory of Decision: New Dimensions of Political Analysis.* Princeton: Princeton University Press, 1974.

Taguieff, P.-A. *Face au racisme.* Paris: La Découverte, 1991.

van der Wurff, A., and P Stringer. "Postvictimization Fear of Crime: Differences in the Perceptions of People and Places, Journal of Interpersonal Violence, Vol. 4, N° 4, 1989." *Journal of Interpersonal Violence.* 4, no. 4 (1989).

Vrij, A., and F. W Winkel. "Characteristics of the Built Environment and Fear of Crime: A Research Note on Interventions in Unsafe Locations." *Deviant Behavior* 12, no. 2 (1991): 203-15.

Wacquant, L. J. D. "Au chevet de la modernité: le diagnostic du docteur Giddens." *Cahiers Internationaux de Sociologie* XCIII (December 1992): 389-97.

Warr, M., and M. Stafford. "Fear of Victimization: A Look at the Proximate Causes." *Social Forces,* 1983: 1033-43.

Weaver, J., and J. Wakshlag. "Perceived vulnerability to crime, criminal victimization experience, and television viewing." *Journal of Broadcasting & Electronic Media* 30, no. 2 (1986): 141-158.

Williams, P, and J. Dickinson. "Fear of Crime: Read All About It?" *British Journal of Criminology* 33, no. 1 (1993).

Windish, U. *Le prêt-à-penser: les formes de la communication et de l'argumentation quotidiennes.* Lausanne: L'Âge d'Homme, 1990.

Winkel, F. W., and A. Vrij. "Fear of Crime and Mass Media Crime Reports: Testing Similarity Hypotheses." *International Review of Victimology* 1, no. 3 (1990): 251-66.

Yanay, U. "The 'Big Brother' Function of Block Watch." *International Journal of Sociology and Social Policy* 14, no. 9 (1994): 45-60.

www.ingramcontent.com/pod-product-compliance
Lightning Source LLC
Chambersburg PA
CBHW030329270326
41926CB00010B/1561